Nickel & Nickel

Best Wishes
for the
Holidays

From your friends at

Far Niente, Dolce and
Nickel & Nickel

Season's Greetings

WINE COUNTRY

WINE
Architecture and Interiors
COUNTRY

MARY WHITESIDES

foreword by Howard J. Backen, FAIA

photography by Matthew Reier

Gibbs Smith, Publisher
Salt Lake City

First Edition

08 07 06 05 04   5 4 3 2 1

Text © 2004 Mary Whitesides
Photography © 2004 Matthew Reier unless otherwise noted

Published by
Gibbs Smith, Publisher
P.O. Box 667
Layton, Utah 84041

Orders: 1.800.748.5439
www.gibbs-smith.com

Designed by Ron Stucki
Printed in Hong Kong

Library of Congress Cataloging-in-Publication Data
Whitesides, Mary.
  Wine country : architecture and interiors / Mary Whitesides.— 1st ed.
     p. cm.
  ISBN 1-58685-464-X
  1. Architecture—California—Napa Valley. 2. Architecture—California—Sonoma
Valley. 3. Interior decoration—United States—California, Northern. I. Title.
NA730.C22N3784 2004
728'.37'097941—dc22
                              2004005058

Contents

Photo by Doug Dun / BAR Architects

Foreword

THERE IS A SIGNIFICANT RELATIONSHIP between architecture and its surroundings that once fully developed will provide evidence of the culture it defines. The wine country region of Napa and Sonoma counties in Northern California has a rich and diverse history that has manifested itself through several distinct architectural styles, each style representing the unique ideals, aspirations, economics, and developmental patterns of its era.

The wine country lifestyle, as presented in the pages of this book, is a reflection of the trends in architectural development within the rural and agricultural lands of Napa and Sonoma counties. Originally influenced by the mission style, rural barn architecture, and European styles associated with the heritage of winemaking, wine country style may be found in both traditional and contemporary designs throughout the area.

Traditional rural designs such as the Nickel & Nickel Winery, the Backen Residence, and the Yountville Barn Style Complex are representative of the early agricultural barns and architecture common in this area. Their forms, materials, and surrounding landscapes reflect their historical precedents.

Creating contemporary design in a rural area presents a unique challenge to the architect. Buildings such as the Quintessa Winery, the Rimerman House, and the Napa Valley Residence are examples of successful contemporary designs that have taken particular consideration in achieving a composition that is true to the heritage of the area and complementary to its surroundings.

In many regions of the country it would seem that such a diverse assortment of architectural styles could present a sort of hodgepodge design consortium. In the wine country regions of the Napa and Sonoma counties, however, this diversity has survived and thrived over the years; it is so captivating in our modern times because each building may be read as a distinct piece of architecture whose style is either complementary to, or conscious of, adjacent structures and their surrounding landscapes. In addition, the development of these areas has been reliant upon the controls instigated by the effective municipalities and building officials

The rich soil in Napa Valley, called serpentine belts, provides perfect conditions for growing grapes similar to those in Tuscany. The Northern California landscape resembles Tuscany, and the emigrants from Italy who settled here influenced its architectural styles.

in the area. In the Napa Valley, development and growth has been controlled by flatland agricultural zoning, and scenic views will be protected by a hillside ordinance that restricts the development of hillsides visible from the valley floor. It is the hope that these ordinances will work together to keep each community distinct and protected against the sort of continuous strip of development that inevitably causes the boundaries of adjacent towns to blend together.

The wine country has preserved its heritage by recognizing the importance of both its natural features and its economic staple—fertile lands and abundant natural resources. The development of architecture in the valley should reflect this, never allowing buildings to be built with zero lot lines, or gated communities to sprout up in areas of open space.

If asked to describe the vernacular of wine country architecture, I cannot pinpoint one specific architectural style, as the essence of the place is truly derived from a rigorous understanding of, and overwhelming affection for, the natural amenities the area provides. The people who inhabit the wine country understand this through experience and allow us to create structures that will flourish as a timeless documentation of architecture that lives happily with the land.

—HOWARD J. BACKEN, FAIA

Acknowledgments

WORKING WITH SOME OF THE FINEST architects in the country for this book has given me a new perspective on the nuances of achievement in architecture. The beautiful homes and wineries found in these pages reflect the creative talent and expertise of professionals living and working in the Napa and Sonoma Valleys. Clients and professionals work together to interpret dreams, fulfill needs, and create responsible buildings to leave on the landscape. The code of building standards in Northern California is one to be studied and from which we can learn.

I would like to thank all the participating architects for their cooperation and generosity in the production of *Wine Country: Architecture and Interiors.* Thank you to architect Howard J. Backen, FAIA, of Backen Gillam Architects for his guidance, suggestions, and partnership in this book. Howard has lived and worked in the Napa Valley for a number of years and fully understands the area's needs and lifestyle. His beautifully designed buildings add to the long-standing heritage of Northern California. I am pleased to have him as the consulting architect on this book.

A special thank you to architect Maurice Lombardo of BTL Architects for the personal interest he took in this project and the time he spent with us during photography sessions. And to Mary Marshall Grace, Director of Communications at Far Niente and Nickel & Nickel Winery, thank you for being so gracious and hospitable. Mike and Toni Doilney, thank you for giving Matt and me a place to stay. It made our job so much easier.

Thank you to the homeowners for sharing their beautiful dwellings with the readers. And to the proprietors of the wineries, thank you for the inspiring architecture found in these pages.

A great big hug goes to my daughter Jessie Whitesides, architect at Backen Gillam Architects—there would not be a book without your help, expertise, and knowledge.

Fresh Food Made Daily
In a hurry? Try our
GRAB
and
GO
ITEMS
to your right

Introduction

"History was born out of a bottle of wine."
—From the vintage film PRISONER OF ZENDA

Comprehensive markets established in Italy during the fifteenth century allowed citizens to purchase fresh food daily. Lack of refrigeration made these markets imperative. In addition, the warmth, conviviality, and ceremonial aspects of the markets established a tradition that citizens of many countries enjoy today. Viansa Winery has created an authentic marketplace as part of the Tuscan experience in their Sonoma County winery.

Wine country style is a gracious, sophisticated way of life carefully developed over decades through agriculture and expressed by architecture. While specialized agriculture is the basis on which the Northern California wine country was built, architecture is the manifestation of the region's prosperity and European legacy. Much of America was developed through agriculture and an architectural heritage, which reaches back into the historical pages of our European roots. But perhaps no other place in the country has developed such a refined blend of both agriculture and architecture as the Napa and Sonoma Valleys in the Northern California wine country.

Embodied in the charm of these Valleys are the lush and fertile lands of a moderate climate that closely resemble the Tuscan countryside where fine wines have been known for hundreds of years. The rich soils of Northern California, called serpentine belts, provide an atmosphere where digger pines, Manzanita, olive trees, and most importantly grape vineyards flourish. The earth erodes quickly in the hills because of deep water that can rise fast and cause landslides. This soil is largely made up of oak litter rich in iron and tannins, ideal conditions for planting and growing vineyards and creating a certain native environment similar to many European vigneron regions.

Over the years, the area has attracted winemaking entrepreneurs from many countries throughout the world. Pioneering agriculturists from Italy, Spain, France, and South America brought with them a diversity of grape species and winemaking methods as well as architectural influences. Many large families coming to the new world from Tuscany chose to settle in the Napa and Sonoma Valleys of California because the climatic conditions were so strikingly similar to their homeland. These families were instrumental in establishing the California wine country as a serious winemaking area. Prominent Italian families still live and participate in the winemaking industry today. A large portion of homes built here are strongly influenced by the Tuscan style farmhouse. Stone buildings with arched doorways, beamed ceilings, gauged plaster walls, warm colors, large kitchens, and outbuildings connected by breezeways are all reminiscent features.

In the early eighteenth century, Spanish monks settled in highly concentrated pockets of California. An important part of the American West was shaped by their efforts. Monks trained and employed the Native Americans in both the value of agriculture and the skill of building. The mission style of the Spanish-influenced buildings in California is beset with a multitude of charming details that beckon romantic images of faraway places. Typically asymmetrical, these buildings feature terra-cotta tiles, stucco surfaces, spiral columns, loggia, boarded window shutters, ornamental metal work, and small balconies. The Spanish Mission buildings were designed and built on a grid system using numerous courtyards that had a crossover aesthetic with the surrounding landscapes. The Spanish created way stations in Northern California where olive groves were planted, maintaining an attitude of harmony with the land.

The strong European influence on wine country style is furthered by the French Chateaux of Normandy. This portion of France, where sought-after wines are produced, established such a grand architectural style when military feudal lords of the fourteenth century were forced to stay in one place. The large fort-like structures they developed from agricultural barns later became the "country castles" of wealthy lords and ladies. Architects of the Renaissance era advanced the look of the chateau with such additions as turrets, gables, circular staircases, and vaulted trussed ceilings. Landscape architecture also developed into an art when gardens were planted by design in precise graphic patterns. A selection of residents in the Napa and Sonoma Valleys have borrowed and imported the French influence into their own discerning wine country lifestyle.

In addition to the strong European heritage of this area, an important portion of the wine country was developed by the American pioneer. California gained notoriety during the gold rush in the mid-1800s. Many miners and pioneers brought with them the humble skills of farming. Farmers regarded their agricultural buildings over and above their own living quarters. The size and style of the barn was a symbol of a prosperous farmer. Their barns and homes reflected the building vernacular of the section of the country from which they came—Victorian style, cottage style, and barn architecture.

Prosperous farmers chose a Victorian-style house where fancy parlor rooms allowed them to entertain as they had in the East. Ornamental elements became a symbol of abundance. Architectural details of the Victorian style include fish-scale facing, curlicue spindled braces, sweeping porches, and large homey kitchens.

The cottage-style house with its low-shingled profile synthesizes well into the agricultural landscape. The subtle, unpretentious patchwork look of these historic farmhouses started humbly with one room. Additional rooms were added on to the structure as the need arose and the budget allowed. Endearing to the warmth and organic look and feel of wine country style, these vintage homes are purchased as renovation projects by people who respect the original intent of the home.

Barn architecture has also been successfully translated into living spaces where the industrial look of massive sliding doors, large contiguous spaces, and an intimate integration with nature is not only a casual, comfortable way to live, but is chic. A simple structure such as this may stand on its own without much ornamentation, but it may also provide the ultimate invitation for personal embellishment. The simplicity of this vernacular is seemingly easily achieved. However, the design-intensive process of making a structure look simple is quite complicated and has not been mastered by many.

Photo by J. D. Peterson

Above: True to the farmhouse architecture of Napa Valley, the soft elegance of outdoor living is showcased by this covered porch connected to the guesthouse. An afternoon gathering is filled with options for a leisurely lunch, a quick dip in the pool, or an engrossing novel.

Center: Although this building resembles a dairy barn, it is actually the main production facility for Nickel & Nickel winery. The architects and owners were adamant that the complex maintain the farming heritage of the Napa Valley. This, the newest structure in the complex, blends easily with the reconstructed vintage Gleason Barn and the renovated Victorian Sullenger House also located on the property.

Far right: This ultimate outdoor room is enclosed by three walls and exposed to nature along the entire length of the backyard perimeter. The oil painting adds an unexpected finesse to the experience of indoor/outdoor living. The room can be closed and locked by lowering a rolling metal door.

Photo by Mary Whitesides

Photo by Mary Whitesides

In the past ten years, a new movement in contemporary architecture has gained momentum. One could call it a hybrid editing of the historical legacy within a certain group of people who simplify their lives by living in a sparse environment. Turning to classic architecture, they look to invite nature into the interior space as part of the design scheme. In this way, the agricultural process is welcome to become a special part of the lives of people who are tenants on the land. Broad, unadorned surfaces where walls open up to the land, double-story windows framing scenic views, and outdoor rooms where the interaction with nature is encouraged all contribute to the evolving contemporary landscape of wine country.

The rich and varied architectural history of the Northern California wine country and the fertile soils that produce abundant vineyards have attracted sophisticated, well-educated people who are conscious of preserving the qualities inherent to the area. The residents of the Napa and Sonoma Valleys understand the fine attributes of well-designed architecture to be the integration of personal taste with the microclimate and history of their surroundings. Today in the wine country, people are passionate about the excellent wines produced in the agricultural region in which they choose to live. The residents look to personalize the architectural forms that express who they are and how they live, while also maintaining the heritage of the area. *Wine Country: Architecture and Interiors* takes an intimate look at the lifestyle of an area of the country that shuns fast food restaurants, billboards, and commercial motels—a lifestyle filled with patient, responsible development and a discriminate way of living.

Yountville Barn
Style Complex

Backen Gillam Architects
Howard J. Backen FAIA, architect
Barbara Colvin, interior designer

Left: Rooms are not segregated boxes in this Yountville residence. Barn architecture dictates one contiguous living area with multipurpose options. Looking from the kitchen, the formal dining room merges with the inviting warmth of the living room where one can easily migrate to the comfort of overstuffed sofas.

Right: Many homes in Northern California feature entire walls that open to the outdoors. This home, designed by architect Howard J. Backen, adopts huge barn-style doors that disappear into metal pockets located on the exterior. The main house is exposed to a sheltered courtyard located between the barn and the house.

Architect Howard Backen's clients had a limited footprint within their land in Yountville, California, where a new home could be built. It was important to them to integrate a living space into their vineyards without disturbing the agricultural fields. This left a slender pad of ground next to the road on which to site the house. Sharing their living space with nature and paying homage to the agricultural heritage of the area were important criteria for them. A rural complex where they could carry on efficiently with the day-to-day business of

Photo by Erhard Pfeiffer

growing grapes was to be integrated with a sophisticated, state-of-the-art living space. With these parameters set, they enlisted Backen's talent. The result is an elegant design that is embraced by the surrounding vineyards.

It is typical of rural homes to be constructed as a series of buildings that form a complex for living, much like a campus. Backen, who is well known for designing simple forms within the vernacular of rural architecture in the Northern California area, was inspired by the clients' desire to explore the essence of their agricultural lands and live within its boundaries without commanding it.

The owners wanted a complex that served their needs in the best possible way, where everyday living would be intermingled with work. The first building in the complex is the barn, which acts as a privacy shield between the road and the main house. Inside the barn is a central entry courtyard flanked by a wide-open storage space for vineyard projects on one side and a charming space used for guest quarters on the other.

Each building in the complex is rectangular in plan and topped with a gable roof. While the exterior materials vary from plaster to wood, the steel sash openings are a constant reminder of the traditional rural barn. All of the buildings open to an interior courtyard by using sliding barn doors. In addition, the main residence opens onto patios and a view of the vineyards through pocket doors that are contained within a steel "shadow box." Pocket doors are typical of Backen's architecture, and have been a

Photo by Erhard Pfeiffer

Below, left: Barn architecture is well suited to wine country. This barn-style structure houses guest quarters on one side, provides storage on the other, shields the main residence from street noise, and provides complete privacy for the owners.

Right: The great room is a third of one contiguous space that includes the dining room and kitchen. A multinational collection of furnishings and materials are used in the interiors. Chipped limestone flooring is imported from India and the fireplace mantel handmade in Italy.

Left: Barbara Colvin, interior designer, was fascinated by the Bauhaus period. The metal-framed sofa filled with soft cushions and pillows is both modern and rustic at the same time, crossing the line between period piece and contemporary living.

Above: Cabinet doors are designed to resemble the structure of a barn door. Sculpted white oak, waxed and dressed with ebonized hardware, maintains the barn look of this Yountville home in a refined way.

Above, right: Within the confined courtyard of this barn-style complex is an outdoor spa. Privacy is assured and nature can be enjoyed without the threat of unexpected intrusion.

part of numerous designs over a period of twenty years. Many of his pocket door systems disappear into a slot routed out between ample walls. The shadow-box system used on this project is a metal casing attached to the exterior, which adds a design element while functioning as a container for the opened doors.

The clients carefully considered their dreams and inspirations for the main house. They analyzed an established lifestyle in order to come up with a design that would maximize how the house fulfilled personal needs. Because compartmentalized subsistence had no appeal, a flexible floor plan inside and out that would change and grow with them became the obvious solution. They were adamant that the home should communicate their passion for work and pleasure, blurring the distinction of usage. To cook, sleep, work, entertain, and relax in one contiguous space suited their lifestyle. Cooking and entertaining go hand-in-hand with wine country living in general and this house is designed to stretch and accommodate a large number of people as well as to nurture a few.

The concept of a great room merging with a spacious kitchen and easy access to the outdoors balances function and form here. The wide-open floor plan is articulated with subtle variations in space usage, where classic European furnishings are transformed by an all-American eclectic inventiveness.

An early-European-style kitchen fits the personalities of the owners, where utensils and small appliances are unabashedly displayed, eliminating the need for upper cabinets. Hard-edge metal appliances contrast with wooden cabinets below the counter, which underwent a five-coat lacquer-and-oil paint process with the shiny surface softened by rubbing with steel wool. Marble was chosen for the warmth of the stone, providing substantially thick counters, a perfect choice to add weight to the kitchen. The patina finishes in this

Photo by Mary Whitesides

kitchen speak of the geniality of Old Europe while the modern stainless-steel Miele appliances make the latest contemporary statement.

Designer Barbara Colvin's enthusiasm for the contrasts between classic, vintage, and modern in her selection of home furnishings seems to cast aside the design boundaries of age and era. Traditional touches add warmth to the house and artfully contemporary accents liven the atmosphere. The classic comforts of overstuffed sofas are accentuated by period pieces, an eighteenth-century mirror sits next to a 1930s metal table, and a contemporary chair is backlit by a seventeenth-century sconce.

Left: A built-in banquette provides an extra option for lounging in the bedroom. The imported French ticking resembles a vintage handmade mattress. A view to the landscape gives pause to contemplate the beauty of the surrounding vineyards.

Far right: A street elevation of this Yountville residence reveals a complex of buildings designed around barn architecture. The ingenious way the architecture is sited provides privacy for the owners and contributes to the agricultural vernacular of the wine country area.

Photo by Mary Whitesides

As an earnest student of art history, Colvin was mesmerized by the colors and patinas of early Italian art, the architecture of the south of France, as well as the modern furniture designs of Bauhaus. She wanted the house to feel like it had a bit of the patina of weathered materials—oxidized metals, natural stones, weathered woods, and plastered walls—without looking forced or contrived. A painting purchased in southern France years ago became the palette of warm neutral linen colors for the entire house, highlighted with bright seasonal accents and trends such as chartreuse and bittersweet orange. At Christmastime, reds and bright pinks are added.

Just as the basic palette for a work of art is the most important decision for an artist, so the flooring, mantels, kitchen counters, and cabinet choices were the most important decisions made in this Yountville residence. The hand-chiseled limestone flooring from India laid throughout the main portion of the house is reminiscent of the early antique floors of Bordeaux. The bedroom floor is recycled two-hundred-year-old walnut from a barn in southern France. The fireplace mantels are a mix of aged and carved limestone, both imported and domestic. In the great room, a massive carved stone French import surrounds the firebox while hand-chiseled limestone fireplaces in the kitchen and bedroom were crafted in Texas.

The exterior materials are singular in coloration throughout the complex with the exception of the paint finish on the barn building, which is dual-toned. Two different paint colors were used: dark olive and khaki. After the paint was applied in layers, a paint remover was dabbed on in random strokes exposing patches of the layer underneath. The resulting aging effect gives the street presentation of the barn a nostalgic look without being ramshackle.

The beauty of simple architecture leaves open the boundless possibilities for personalization. With or without embellishment this well-designed and well-executed barn-style complex is timeless. Vernacular architecture such as this residence exhibits the expertise of architect Howard Backen, who over the years has mastered the intricate art of simplicity. The complete complement of exterior and interior spaces makes this Yountville home a successful partnership between client and architect.

2

French Manor House Chateau

Brandenburger Taylor Lombardo Architects, LLP

Ken Poisson, Les Poisson Interiors

Brandenburger Taylor Lombardo Architects have designed a French chateau in the hills of the California wine country that is so authentic, one is transported to the vineyards of France. The marriage of Normandy architecture and modern living was a union brought together by the hopes and dreams of the owners and extensive research by the architects. The designers, fulfilling the capacious imagination of their clients, have accomplished the lofty task with great bravado.

Chateau literally means "castle" in French, and if a man's home is his castle, the definition may be interpreted literally here. This home is an exemplary typological model of the chateaux of the

Left: The turrets of chateau architecture once served the feudal lords of France as lookouts for military maneuvers. Translated here in the guesthouse, the turret is used as a gathering place for grandchildren who may want to keep a lookout for parents and grandparents.

Right, above: The entrance to this home is a classic arch constructed of wedge-shaped stones and marked by a keystone at the apex. This curved structure was commonly used over a doorway for structural stability as well as aesthetics. The cabriole leg table in the entrance is a very rare seventeenth-century French antique.

Right, below: An oval window like this, called an oculus in classic architecture, was commonly used in walls or domes. This eye-shaped window located in the hallway allows a peek into the garden before entering the living room.

Photo by Mary Whitesides

Normandy region. The original archetype of the chateau is derived from the castle fortifications established by powerful military men in the ninth century. The fortifications compelled these military feudal lords to stay in one place and develop land rather than constantly being on the march in military maneuvers. They tied themselves to the land by developing vineyards as their primary agricultural crop. Thus the chateau has become a symbol of the vineyard. This social stability secured the position of these castle fortifications in architectural history. From the ninth century and over a period of a thousand years, the architecture evolved from fortress into chateau and came to be revered as the residences of French nobility.

The owners of this home are drawn to the French countryside as though they intuitively belong there. With the spirit of investigation, they enthusiastically researched chateau architecture and period furnishings. Returning with an imagination teeming with ideas, they brought their dreams to the architects.

The design is precise in every detail, executed by an army of Napa Valley craftsmen that the world thought lost. All materials pertinent to the look of the home were imported from France, including windows, doors, roof tiles, stone details, and paneling. Rare antique furniture, rugs, fabrics, and paintings personally selected by the owners and their interior designer, Ken Poisson of Les Poisson Interiors, were shipped from France as well. From the outstanding cultural landscape of France, a historic aesthetic has been preserved and brought forward to function in the Napa Valley.

The architects carefully nestled the home on the mountain site, offering its inhabitants expansive views of the Napa Valley. This extremely refined home is a series of towers, squares, and corridors radiating from a central rectangular barn shape. Combinations of gable, hip, and cone roofs flow together, containing the floor plan under one contiguous lid. French tiles end gracefully in flared eaves over a series of shuttered windows, with the steep slope of the roof interrupted by gables. Thick stucco walls resemble the load-bearing masonry construction of medieval times. Truncated wedge-shaped stones form a horseshoe casing around arched walnut doors leading to a grand entrance hall. Once inside the hall, it is clear that this is the point at which the social hubbub

Below, left: A private conversation area is located in a corner of the great room. The painting, upholstery fabrics, and lighting coin a setting much like one to be found in a French chateau.

Below, right: The grandeur of the entrance hall is enhanced by French antiques, sconces, and chandeliers. White marble floors are classically inlaid with black marble, and the vintage beams give architectural presence to the room.

Right: From the entrance, guests may exit through draped French doors to a large courtyard with seating around an outdoor fireplace and rambling views of Napa Valley. Other rooms also have access to this courtyard.

Photo by Mary Whitesides

Photo by Mary Whitesides

and tranquil retreat of the home come together. Successions of rooms circulate from this center point: public areas to the left and private rooms to the right.

The public spaces to the left begin with the living room where a small oval window framed in stone draws one to peek at the garden just before entering. Exposed hand-hewn trusses supporting a vaulted ceiling define the living room. At the apex above the entrance, a Juliet balcony oversees a comprehensive selection of antique French furnishings. Germane to the period, wood parquet flooring in a Versailles pattern sets the background for all the appointments in the house.

The formal dining room mimics a simplified version of Versailles. Stunning three-hundred-year-old

creamy green paneling has aged gracefully. If only these walls could talk, what stories would be told. This room is adorned with gilt side tables, bronze sconces, and sweeping draperies, prompting dinner guests to fancy themselves distinguished time travelers in a manor befitting nobility.

Nothing but a La Cornue cooking range would do in an extraordinary French country kitchen of this magnitude. The old adage "too many cooks in the kitchen" does not apply in a space like this. A sizable carved limestone hood and bold hand-painted tiles maintain accurate proportion with the size of the room. Scrupulously sensitive to the period, the cabinets echo the palette and motif of the antique paneling in the dining room. A classic pewter rod-and-latch system operates the stacked windows.

The flow of traffic and the use of soft colors in the public wing liberate the mind and soul. Wide pocket terraces spill out of a series of French doors, and expansive glass walls invite the outdoors in. Unrestricted quarters allow one to move freely about and invest in conversations with a generosity of spirit and friendship reminiscent of those fostered over a glass of fine wine at a chateau in medieval times.

Only in the use of materials and temperature control does the wine cellar

Photo by Mary Whitesides

in this contemporary chateau differ from ancient cellars. The provocative and reverberating ribbed pattern of the vaulted groin-style ceiling is a construction technique that challenges the skills of today's finest engineers even though it dates back hundreds of years.

In contrast to the public areas, the private rooms have been treated with a dark color scheme to codify the mood and encourage leisurely activities. In the library, ancient oak paneling—a three-hundred-year-old artifact imported from France—lines the walls. Whether you are there to read, think, take in a film, or write a letter, this room is the place to liberate the mind and invite the muse. A game table is set near the warmth of an elegant wood-burning marble-fronted fireplace, and a writing desk sits before a window from which to gaze. Off the library, a small narrow hallway leads to the master suite. A grand circular limestone staircase fabricated in France is topped by a domed wooden spandrel and rises to a second bedroom, a private office, and the Juliet balcony.

The design of this Napa Valley chateau is the kind of enthralling project that tests the inventive mind of an architect. Clearly Brandenburger Taylor Lombardo's assessment of the French chateau is precisely executed in every detail. Through expertise, communication, interaction, and imagination, a French chateau that fulfills the heart's desire of the owners and the rare opportunity to unbridle an architect's yearning for the "dream job" was realized.

Far left: The landscaping provides shelter, beauty, and privacy for the home. An elevation of the main house is seen through the grounds, which are groomed and choreographed like a French garden. Hidden amongst the gardens are paths that lead to a pool, tennis courts, and patios.

Left: A carved angelic icon is called an alto-rilievo, meaning high relief. Such sculptural elements were found in French gardens and on patios as a popular form of decorative art during the Renaissance.

Right: This ultimate French country kitchen is large enough to encourage more than one cook to participate in food preparation. The finish work on the cabinets is carefully colorized to harmonize with the three-hundred-year-old paneling found in the dining room. The large windows are opened and closed with a classic pewter rod-and-latch system.

Harris House Compound

French Mediterranean
Geyserville, California

Marc and Peggy Harris took seven years to build their family compound on a remote mountaintop near Geyserville, California. Located north of Healdsburg, Geyserville is in the heart of Sonoma County wine country. With stewardship over hundreds of acres, the Harrises felt it was important to introduce dwellings that look like they have always belonged there. To accomplish this, Peggy defined the living area by connecting the surrounding landscape with outdoor garden rooms. Marc based his design of the dwellings on the selection of plant species and their configuration on the land. The resulting building materials are all highly respectful of the outstanding beauty of the environment.

Because the Harrises like to live their lives in stages, they segregated their

A sense of arrival is established at the Harris home by a breezeway. The house is divided into two sections: entrance to the kitchen is on the right, and entrance to the living room/private wing is on the left. Outdoor dining is also an option where lawn meets patio, and views of the Alexander Valley are spectacular.

property into five sections, studying each intently until it was clear what was to be built where. Developing a complex of buildings that evolves innately from the characteristics of the landscape takes ingenuity, patience, and persistence. The Harrises began with a modest cottage, later to become the guesthouse, in which they lived while fulfilling their lifelong dream. An emphasis was placed on an authentic natural look with an honest use of materials. This, along with a commitment to sweat equity, allowed the cottage to be built on a modest budget, while determination and imagination led the owners to accomplish their goals.

Limestone flooring was high on the list of materials but not within the modest budget. Not willing to concede their design aesthetic to budgetary constraints, the Harrises cast their own floor tile with a faux finish, maintaining the inherent tone and texture of limestone. Success emboldened them to continue. Knowing they would live in less than 1,000 square feet with two sons for a number of years, simple spaces were key—nothing too excessive or extravagant. Prudent decisions made the cottage distinctly personal and

Photo by Mary Whitesides

Photo by Mary Whitesides

livable for the family, but a second structure served a critical need for space to entertain and to house their large collection of artifacts from around the world.

Being mindful of the area's agricultural history helped determine the size, form, and aesthetic of a stunning red barn. Mixing elements from favorite worldly places with the reality of the wine country environment served as the philosophy for this expressive building. One wide-open vaulted space accommodates a lengthy dining table where friends and family linger over a gourmet meal, surrounded by ornate architectural artifacts from India and Indonesia. With each new building, the Harrises added a new dimension to their lives and meaning to their land.

To unleash the creative process for the main house, the couple took an interesting approach. They gathered Sonoma fieldstone with a specific palette in mind, painstakingly sorting through tons of rock for color and fracture. Laying out stone walls to create terraces, they let the rock define the spaces for the house and its outbuildings, a massive doghouse, and a laundry facility. Working a pattern with the fieldstone, they used cobbles and moss-covered rock to delineate the final motif.

The main house took on a French Mediterranean style with a rectangular plan and a living bridge, an

outdoor hallway that forms a cleft between social and utilitarian functions. This arched ambulatory entrance draws one to a view of the Alexander Valley before making a choice to step into the kitchen on the left or living room on the right. All rooms in the two-story house open visually onto the landscape from a balcony or into the garden through French doors.

Reclaimed materials support the organic look and feel essential to this dwelling. Marinated wine-vat staves with deep variegated tones clad the upper portion of the façade, contrasted by the stucco surface of the foundation. Spanish terra-cotta tiles salvaged from a razed building add patina to the roof. Cast-concrete slab flooring, easily mistaken for genuine limestone, is used throughout the main house.

The color scheme for the interiors was not selected from paint chips at the local paint store but derived from the natural palette of the environmental surroundings. With a white piece of paper in hand, Marc Harris gathered oak litter and soil with a high content of manganese and serpentine. Organic materials from the property were used to determine colors compatible with the landscape.

Marc created a plaster color that looked

Left: A view from the breezeway into the kitchen reveals the open look of this room. The outdoors is accessed from the room in three directions. French doors lead to an open patio with a state-of-the-art barbeque, another set of doors lead directly onto the lawn, and a third set to the breezeway. The floors resemble limestone but are faux textured concrete.

Right: Located on the property is a small guesthouse. The Harrises lived in this 1,000-square-foot house for a number of years while designing and building their dream home. The bedroom is one of three rooms. Marc Harris designed the iron bedstead that was handmade in Mexico.

Photo by Mary Whitesides

Photo by Mary Whitesides

right with the indigenous oak trees, digger pines, madrones, and olive trees. To a soft umber plaster, he added green oxide for an aged texture and enhanced color. The wet plaster was alarmingly intense, but the curing process mellowed the finish. Marc discovered that choosing what color was to go on which wall was difficult, as the tone tends to change according to the light. On a lit wall he used less pigment; on a shadowed wall, more pigment. For the final finish, a mixture of plaster, watered down, was applied with a squeegee.

Through tenacity, sensitivity to the land, and reverence for the history of Northern California, the Harrises have transformed reality into personal imagination. They took their time, allowing the creative process to unfold in stages and to question the reason for what they built. How to express what personally inspires can mean the difference between imitation and originality. After seven years as colonizers in the mountains of the wine country, the Harrises now live the life they have dreamed of.

4

Villa Pietra ("Stone House")

Tuscan Farmhouse

Brandenburger Taylor Lombardo Architects, LLP

Left: The Palladian symmetry of this Tuscan home in Sonoma Valley is apparent. The main windows in the living room are spaced precisely beneath the upper portal windows. The furnishings adhere to the geometry of the space and colors are chosen for tonal qualities and warmth.

Right: A gallery of columns lines the U-shaped design of this house. Flanking each side of the common porch are two private porches accessed through the master suite on the right side and the guest wing on the left side. The U-shape forms a natural courtyard planted in grass.

An ancient philosophy states that life should permeate nature and give substance to celestial bodies. A hillside site with exceptional views overlooking mountains and valley vineyards is the dream location for a house that honors this philosophy. Architectural plans for such a house were finalized and ready for construction when a problem arose. A monumental bed of rock lay just beneath the surface of the planned foundation. Blasting to excavate the extreme density of this stone was the only answer and left no doubt the home was built on a solid foundation. Fortunately, this did not deter Brandenburger Taylor

Lombardo Architects; it simply made their job more interesting.

The owner's strong Italian heritage and the Sonoma wine country evoked the style of the house: a Tuscan villa with a sunny California overlay. The straightforward architectural presentation captures the imagination much like the elementary rectangular houses drawn by a child, but alludes to something more. Even though the house looks as if it is a simple geometric form, it is full of surprising details.

The front entrance, marked by an arched cast-stone casing surrounding bronze double doors, is the center of a perfect symmetry for the entire plan. Stone box sills encase stained-wood windows imported

Left: The kitchen, located in one great space across from the living room, provides an option to sit at the counter for casual meals or at an adjoining dining room table for formal dining. The tremendous range hood is an architectural feature that adds a defining element to the kitchen.

Right: A double row of twin columns delineates the gallery that runs the length of the house. Located on each end of the gallery are comfortable seating areas—one near a fireplace configured like a yawning lion's mouth (see page 14), and the other near a statuette in a niche. A centrally located tile table with cushioned iron chairs offers another intimate gathering spot.

from Italy. Carved stone flanks each side of the door. Portico windows on the upper floors soften the appearance of a stone-wall façade. Both sets of windows, upper and lower, define the symmetry of the design. The building skin dressed with stone appears to be standard masonry from a distance. Upon closer inspection, improvisational patterns are revealed. Shaved pieces of terra-cotta barrel tiles and a series of other bar shapes are inserted into the stonework in flared, stacked, and herringbone motifs. Randomly located throughout the facing, the artistic impact deepens the appreciation of the craftsmanship. The buttery yellow stone used on the house came from a quarry in

Photo by Mary Whitesides

Oklahoma where each piece was inspected for tone and compatibility.

The key element of Brandenburger Taylor Lombardo's design is understanding how the users move from one part of the house to another. Nothing is static in this design. The circulation route provides access around the building through a carefully considered sequence. The living room, dining room, and kitchen join together in a fusion of spaces running through the central grand entrance. A smorgasbord of comforts is an open invitation for family and

Far left: The beautifully crafted stone chimneys of this home add design detail to the architecture. Rooftop pavilions are common features in Tuscan architecture, and a staircase from the gallery below provides access to this version in the Sonoma Valley.

Left: A celestial orb hangs from the arched ceiling in the master bathroom where the shower is located beyond the French doors. A double sink designed by the architects is formed by an undulating wave of metal. The metal-based tub is curved to conform to the human body.

Right: In the master suite, four walls rise to a vaulted quadrangle and form a ceiling burnished with gold gilt. A Saturn-shaped fixture hangs from the center where four hips meet. Embossed flowers give textural interest to the fireplace surround.

friends to feel at home. On the left, luscious tangerine-colored sofas hug an enormous wood-burning stone fireplace in the living room. On the right, umber plaster walls warm the Tuscan kitchen, characterized by a sizable range hood, dark rich cabinets overhung by cooking pots, and an island counter. Off to one side of the kitchen, the home fires are kept burning in another fireplace with a raised wood-burning oven.

Two private bedroom wings branch off either side of this commodious common space helping to frame a view to the exterior portico. The master suite is secluded; it's found down a hallway off the kitchen while the guest area is located off the living room. In the master suite, four walls rising to a vaulted quadrangle form a celestial-like ceiling burnished with gold gilt. A Saturn-like fixture hangs from the center where four hips meet. Flowers embossed on the concrete fireplace mantel add textural interest to the exuberantly decorated room.

The master bath decorously follows suit. Two connected sinks are sensuously formed by an undulating curve of metal and set below the counter surface, specifically designed for the project by the architects. Mosaic tiles form a

backsplash and add color and design. The curvature of the tub mimicking the sensuously formed sinks accommodates the graceful curves of the human body. Horseshoe-arched doors lead to an outdoor shower, and a glowing milk-glass ball with an orb of metal moodily lights this private spa.

The guest bedrooms located off the living room have a compatible identity with the house and share in the comforts of fine linens and fluffy comforters. The colors are variations of warm tones ranging from umber to tangerine to rust. One bedroom has a distinct bathroom. The bathtub/shower, enveloped by a Moroccan-inspired, key-shaped arch, is tiled in small golden glass squares.

Perhaps the most compelling detail in the house is the set of glass pocket doors that run the length

of the house. One entire wall can disappear into side slots, exposing the common space to nature through the covered portico formed by a sequence of custom-designed columns. A tile-encrusted table surrounded by cushioned metal chairs separates two other seating areas in this gallery space: one side huddles the fireplace, which is carved like a roaring lion's mouth in bas-relief; the other side clusters near a large niche displaying a bronze statue. Two galleries leading away from each side of the portico down the length of the private wings end in identical square porches. The resultant U-shaped footprint is filled with lawn and garden. Following the sprawl of lawn down the central line that forms the axis of the entire plan, there is an infinity pool. Two matching glass-enclosed pool houses await the swimmer from either end. A bocce court area marks the edge of the property with a touch of Italian culture. Looking back along a great stretch of lawn onto the sunny yellow stone house lined with its row of ionic columns, the romance of Tuscan-style architecture can be appreciated in its entirety.

Brandenburger Taylor Lombardo maintains a rhythmic geometry in the design of this Tuscan-style house without sacrificing spontaneity. It is impossible to find one surface, color, texture, or material that doesn't work with the theme. Built of stone and sited on a stone foundation, this structure is here to stay, one that future generations will appreciate just as it is appreciated today.

5 Rimerman House

Contemporary Architecture
Jim Jennings, architect

The Napa Valley is a most unlikely place to find a Miesian Box—an architectural concept based on two simple ideas: (1) glass/masonry filling for walls, or skin; and (2) steel frames, or the skeleton. As a pioneer in glass skyscrapers, Mies Van der Rohe used this idea in 1938 to mark a sophisticated new direction for urban building design. Not many would choose to build a modern home based on this concept in the Napa Valley countryside; but a glass box that can be cold and impersonal in the concrete jungle of a city provides an opportunity to collude with nature when sited in the woods.

Left: The dining room and living room are composed of one rectangular length. The glass walls are defined in contemporary architecture as the "skin" and the steel frames as the "skeleton." Two opposing walls of glass allow nature and light to pass through the house changing its character as the sun shifts position throughout the day.

Right, top: Contemporary art is hung throughout the house. Owner Tom Rimerman placed individual works of art on the schematic drawings during the design phase. Art and living space now merge beautifully where natural light, size, and shape of walls flow with the layout from room to room.

Right, bottom: Soothing dark colors have a calming effect in the kitchen so that meals are prepared in a meditative atmosphere. The black granite countertop has been honed to eliminate the shiny surface. The cabinets are made of Macaré wood. An unusually shaped stainless steel range hood adds a sculptural element to the design.

Tom and Gayle Rimerman lived and worked on the San Francisco Peninsula for a number of years before moving north to the wine country. As lovers of contemporary architecture and collectors of modern art, they wanted a house that itself would become a sculpture amongst the trees. Their unfettered vision of a contemporary house with plenty of natural light and open space became reality through the design work of architect Jim Jennings. His unassuming architecture clearly expresses this vision in a functional and efficient design where natural environment and man-made materials are composed in harmony. One might say

he has created a design that visually allows nature to run through it. The Rimermans wanted a house that would become a part of their site, embodying the elegance of its natural surroundings.

The house has a very private approach of more than a mile through a natural forest. The strictly unadorned surface at the entrance makes no suggestion of the intimate play between house and woods. Just inside the door, an alcove window leads the eye to a courtyard of trees invited in as part of the art and architecture. Hanging on each side of the entry walls are large Sol Lenitt monotypes.

The Rimermans wanted a homogenous plan where rooms connect one with another as seamless as a symphony played by a well-practiced orchestra. Jennings captured the clients' ideal with the embodiment of one free-flowing L-shaped space where exterior portions of the house can be viewed from the interior. The house is built on five levels. Maintaining a consistent roofline, each floor level has been manipulated to accomplish a varied ceiling height and allow exterior access on grade. A sense of scale is established by a panorama of steel-framed windows that are high enough to withstand the mass of trees caressing the house and broad enough to take in the valley views. All rooms in the house have a glass curtain of windows.

The master bedroom is so simply articulated and so privately situated in the woods that window coverings are unnecessary. A clear mind and a good night's rest are assured for lack of clutter. Even the shower shares a window wall with the outdoors, giving a refined sense of primitive freedom.

A length of bathroom mirrors reflects a gallery of Jean DuBuffet paintings, making them doubly appreciated. Because art

Below: A wooden platform is constructed on the edge of the hill unembellished by stairs, railings, or barbeques. A simple seating arrangement provides a spot in the trees to sit and contemplate the sunset over the valley and vineyards below.

Right: Every room in the Rimerman house has a curtain of glass. Draperies are unnecessary as privacy is not an issue: all views are oriented toward the woods away from public entrances.

throughout the house is placed with such distinction one might deduce that the architect planned the spaces around the Rimerman's art collection. Quite the contrary. Tom began locating the paintings in the house during the schematic design phase. He sought to take advantage of space, light, and views, allowing the art to also be seen from the outside looking in.

Complete symmetry sweeps the main portion of the house in one tremendous glass box where windows span two sides of the living room. This Miesian "skin" starts at the dining room and ends at the

entrance to a private study. Hanging above the fireplace, a fiery red abstract painting fills the room with energy. On one side of the living room, the view filters through the trees and falls off into the vast Napa Valley. On the other, substantial sliding glass doors open onto a patio where the eye is directed back toward the architecture of the private bedroom wing.

A play of light and shadows changes the dialogue of exterior and interior spaces throughout the day. Early morning twilight mellows the geometric angles. The harsh noontime sun strikes the windows with an

Left: Sunset emits an ethereal radiance in the living room. An amber glow bathes the angular furniture and the room takes on a diaphanous quality.

Below, left: The Rimerman's wanted the site to dictate what their house would be. Although building a contemporary home in the Napa Valley woods is an unusual concept, their house shows the versatility of modern architecture. It is like taking a museum and putting it in a forest. Because of the choice of color and the way the house is sited and structured, it suits the landscape.

Below, right: Even though this wine cellar is small in square footage, it is so efficiently designed the storage capacity is enormous. Each slot is precisely configured to tilt the wine bottle at just the right angle.

illusion of opacity. Late afternoon light floods the house with a velvet array of golden sunbeams.

From the outdoors, reflections of trees, gardens, lounges, and plant containers paint a mutable abstraction on the glass. A murmuring sound of water gently steers the mind toward a lap pool pointing directly at the guesthouse, which shares the same lyricism of simplicity as the main house but on a smaller scale. The square guesthouse is stretched two stories high to accommodate a sleeping loft. Slabs of glass connect the foundation with the roofline and promote a free exchange with nature. There is such clarity in this most elemental of forms.

Architect Jim Jennings creatively redefines the architectural basics of the Miesian box: glass, steel, iron, and concrete. Distinct vision, pure intent, and precise geometric planning set this contemporary house apart and allow the trees to find an unassuming new playmate.

6 | Quintessa Winery

Rustic Contemporary Architecture

Walker Warner Architects
Brooks Walker, principal architect in charge

Left: The waiting room at Quintessa Winery is a study in contrasts. Even though it is a commercial enterprise, the room has a homey appeal brought out by the leather chairs, fireplace, and unique light fixture. The concrete walls contrast nicely with the stone fireplace and the halo effect of the chandelier warms the space.

Right: Stepping from the multistoried waiting room into a cave-like space, one enters the tasting room at Quintessa. The public is invited to sit at a table where the ambient glow of backlit paintings creates an atmosphere of intimacy. The torchiere lights were designed specifically for this room.

S et back from the Silverado Trail in Napa Valley and nestled into a hillside, the symmetrically ascending crescent form of the Quintessa Winery comes alive each morning at sunrise. Nature's light show on this architectural amphitheater embraces its vineyards in the early morning hours as a great theater embraces a captivated audience with a masterful performance; here, it is the performance of wine making.

Quintessa, derived from the word quintessential, means "the essence of a thing in its purest and most concentrated form." The name was a calculated choice meant to serve as a business philosophy and a mission statement for the architects.

Photo by Mary Whitesides

Photo by Richard Barnes

Walker Warner Architects faced a unique challenge in creating a state-of-the-art wine-making facility that could stand up to the meaning of its name. They began by paying special attention to the constraints of the site and roadway presentation, and complemented this with function and efficiency.

From the road the building appears as an elegant curved stone wall inset by one simple portal of glass doors leading to the wine caves and wine-making operations.

The sensuous curve of the sculptural wall is clad with a blend of stone types, including local tufa rock, and grouted with a mixture of pea gravel, in a simple rustic style. The hospitality functions are in the

Left, top: Architect Brooks Walker let the site dictate the shape and function of the building. Here the entrance to the hospitality area of the winery sits atop a hillside above the production facility.

Left, bottom: The steel frame or "skeleton" of the building forms a corner for the clerestory windows in the waiting room. A shed roof protects the room from harsh radiant sun by mollifying the light source.

Right: The tasting room is a study in contrasts. Smooth concrete walls meet a textured concrete floor. Wood, steel, and leather not only set off the hard edge surfaces with deep colors, but also invite the human element to become part of the room.

main building, a rectangular configuration of multiple ceiling heights tucked against the hillside atop the arc of the sculptured wall. Constructed of steel and glass in contrast to the stone wall, one form offsets the other respectively, maintaining a separate integrity.

The reception area centrally located in the main building rises above two adjoining wings. Clerestory windows dress the simplistic concrete walls. Steel beams crossing in front of the corner windows candidly express the contemporary design language. An originally designed chandelier is a halo of textured glass, the crowning glory of the room.

Adjacent to the reception area is the tasting room where a common space accommodates individual tasters. The mood here is directed by backlit paintings that cast a diaphanous glow onto walnut tables and leather stools. Ground concrete floors are in textural contrast to smooth concrete walls and a crosshatched concrete countertop. Elemental light fixtures are lucid markers for intimate

nooks where a glass of wine can be sampled. Quintessa also hosts group connoisseurs in a cave-like chamber where wine is ceremoniously uncorked and tasted.

A private tour of the facility will reveal that the architects, with the help of Quintessa's winemaker, have composed the buildings in such a way as to allow the wine-making

process to be returned to its purist form. By utilizing the hillside they are able to gravity-feed the "must" into the fermentation tanks, eliminating the need for any mechanical pumping.

At Quintessa the wine is barrel-aged in French oak and stored in 17,000 square feet of man-made caves. Four cavernous corridors, which make up the spines of the caves merge into a spherical anteroom with a stone obelisk fountain as the focal point. Another textured-glass chandelier casts an aureole of light on the wall like giant luminous clouds.

Quintessa winery is a study in contrasts, joining contemporary design with traditional skills, mass with minimalism, arcs with squares, concrete with wood, and texture with burnished surfaces. Walker Warner Architects achieves a yin-yang balance harmonious with nature and concordant with function.

Photo by Glen Graves

7 | Nickel & Nickel Winery Complex

*Brandenburger Taylor Lombardo
Architects, LLP*

As earnest custodians of the Oakville, California, farming legacy, the Nickel family is dedicated to preserving the imagery and psychological impact this heritage has had on the landscape and architecture of the area. Agriculture has played a huge role in the development of America. In 1830, settlers who began a farming tradition here found that the rich, fertile soils were perfect for growing grapes. Conditions were so ripe for prosperity that it inspired building complexes to suit a newly established lifestyle. The Nickel & Nickel winery pays tribute to that agricultural and architectural history. Planned as a cluster of farm buildings—including a reconstructed hay barn, a restored farmhouse, and a newly designed fermentation barn—this modern facility is a pristine complex that has captured the

essence of each building's heyday while maintaining an unpretentious charm.

The Gleason Barn
Vintage Barn

The newest structure on the site is actually the oldest. The administrative offices of Nickel & Nickel are located in The Gleason Barn, originally built circa 1770 in Meriden, New Hampshire. It was once a home to farm animals.

This Revolutionary War–era hay barn,

which was slated to be razed at the time of purchase by the late Gil Nickel, was moved west instead. In doing this he faced a myriad of noteworthy circumstances revolving around the dismantling of the barn and reassembling it in a different state under different building codes. Notably, the changes in building codes from 1770 to 2003 presented a problem for reassembling the structure exactly, but Brandenburger Taylor Lombardo Architects were able to meet the strict seismic codes in California through innovative engineering during reconstruction. It took a total of two years to methodically dismantle and reconstruct The Gleason Barn without destroying the integrity and finish of the materials. The barnwood siding is in remarkable condition after being exposed to the elements for many years. The exterior siding was originally painted "barn red," as remnants of color remain after exposure to harsh weather. The allure of this aged character would challenge any faux painter's brush. In contrast, and as relief from the naturally distressed exterior, the newly painted contemporary French doors give a fresh look to the façade, creating a solid statement for the entrance.

Far left: Two grain silos stand as landmarks at the Nickel & Nickel winery complex. Made of corrugated metal, they are strikingly contemporary in contrast to the more than two-hundred-year-old Gleason Barn. The two towers can be spotted from a distance when traveling on Highway 29 through Oakville.

Left: The Revolutionary–era hay barn that is now part of the Nickel & Nickel winery complex had to be reengineered to meet strict seismic codes for California. Even though the beams are more than two hundred years old, they remain strong and supportive. The bottom level of this facility plays host to public inquiries while the upper-loft area contains the administrative offices.

Right: At Nickel & Nickel this New Hampshire barn (known as the Gleason Barn) was reconstructed so skillfully that it looks to have been originally built on the site. The siding, once painted red, is weatherworn to a patina that defies a painter's brush.

Once inside, it becomes clear that the architectural structure of the interiors remains true to the period in which it was built, while the function of the barn has been adapted to its current demands as the winery administration building. A network of original hand-hewn beams hacked from pine and hemlock is still visible in the pitched ceiling. The preserved timeworn woods are the perfect embodiment of the warmth of the era. Nails, screws, and brackets are not found in the structure, as the wood-pegged, post-and-beam construction

method of 1770 was once again used to reassemble the barn. The hayloft and animal stalls, now enclosed in glass, house the administrative offices. On the main floor, the laboratory, also enclosed in glass, facilitates an open view throughout the space.

Materials and technologies compressed over a period of three centuries gives The Gleason Barn a new purpose while preserving agricultural history in the form of barn architecture. This image of the Early American farming industry stands as a page out of history that now represents the modern wine industry.

Left: The Gleason Barn pays homage to the agricultural legacy of Northern California. Much of America was developed by the farming industry, and wine country continues that tradition—by working the land and through its adherence to barn architecture.

Right: The Sullenger House is a historic landmark in Oakville, California. Now part of the Nickel & Nickel winery complex, it serves as the hospitality facility. Winery functions are hosted at this newly renovated Victorian house. Even though it looks plain, there are subtle entablatures such as fish scale trim, sunburst brackets, and rosettes.

The Sullenger House

Victorian Manor Queen Anne Style
Architectural Resources Group
Candra Scott & Anderson, Interior Design

When the Nickels purchased the century-old Sullenger house, it was a historic landmark in Oakville, California, and had been abandoned for two decades. After such a long period of neglect, the owners employed Architectural Resources Group to update this grand old Queen Anne while maintaining the identity of the period architecture. For Nickel & Nickel this gracious piece of nostalgic architecture is the key calling card for the winery complex. Fully visible from Highway 29, the newly restored farmhouse serves as the hospitality anchor where wine tasting, dinners, and presentations take place.

The Sullenger House celebrates the graceful charms of Victorian times in a simplified form. Rococo embellishments endemic to this Americanized style of architecture can still be found here but in a more subtle way. From a distance the architecture appears unadorned; upon closer inspection, subtle entablatures such as fish-scale trim, sunburst brackets, and rosettes offset the simple clapboard siding.

Candra Scott and Anderson, Interior Design, took a preservationist attitude toward the interiors, mixing traditional Victorian antiques with an unexpected color scheme. Inviting shades of peach, soft blues, and buttery yellows revive the interiors, making historical appointments savvy in a contemporary world. French mantels with mirrored trumeau and tiles from the 1920s focus the parlor and dining room. Colors and patterns achieved on the fireplace tiles cannot be duplicated today, as browns are especially difficult to maintain during the firing process. Beaded ropes that drape across trendy sconces flank the mirrors, and one-of-a-kind crystal chandeliers provide the main light source.

The Old World opulence of these character-filled rooms honors the era of the original owner, John C. Sullenger, while presenting a freshened Victorian look suitable for the modern hospitality needs of the Nickel & Nickel winery. The Sullenger House is given a new life of which the previous owner would have been proud.

The Fermentation Barn

Dairy Barn Architecture
Brandenburger Taylor Lombardo Architects, LLP

The final piece of the Nickel & Nickel complex is the newly constructed fermentation barn, which appropriately houses the most modern and up-to-date wine-making functions as well as the barrel-storage accommodations. The design, in keeping with the period of The Gleason Barn and the Sullenger House, is made of century-old timbers assembled according to the architectural vernacular and the client's spatial and technical needs for producing wine. Although the building is precisely constructed to operate in the twenty-first century, it was assembled out of a mixture of old and new

Below: Fermentation is one of the most critical steps in the wine-making process. Temperature and timing are controlled in the tanks by the winemaker to achieve the right blend of tannins for the kind of wine desired. In the fermentation barn at Nickel & Nickel, the technical aspects can easily be checked on a catwalk.

Right: The newest addition to the Nickel & Nickel winery complex may resemble a dairy barn but is actually a very technically advanced fermentation barn. The board-and-batten siding is painted white, inspired by a separate vintage barn on the property. With a stone base, the underground wine storage can easily maintain the proper temperature.

timbers that were put together by 400 wooden pegs, or trunnels, driven by a wooden mallet known as a bee-tle. Care was obviously taken to respect the building methods and aesthetics of the other two buildings on site. Judging from the form of the fermentation barn, the brightly painted façade, and a series of gables, one might be expecting to walk into a new dairy barn.

Photo by Mary Whitesides

But reflective steel fermentation tanks full of wine have replaced the dairy cow and her milk. An aluminum staircase leads to a sizable catwalk providing access to the tanks. A commanding vaulted ceiling of corrugated metal seemingly floating above dark, rich walnut beams polarizes the space against the steel tanks.

After a tour of the magnanimous wine cellar below, the people at Nickel & Nickel winery invite their guests into the production facility for tasting. Ostensibly endless aisles of barrels are meticulously laid out on the cellar floor. The walls are finished with a soft umber-colored, hard-troweled plaster, and the lighting in the vaulted groin ceiling sets the mood one would expect to find in an underground cellar. This tour is the perfect opportunity for the visitor to become uniquely familiar with the Nickel & Nickel wine-making process in a building that reflects the agricultural history of the area.

These three historic buildings accommodate Nickel & Nickel's needs in the contemporary wine-making industry. The exciting blend of architectural styles stems from different periods in time but is part of the same agricultural past. Each building with its own identity and historical background contributes to the overall feeling of the American saga. The administrative facilities, housed in The Gleason Barn with its 250 years of history, sits near the hospitality center in the Sullenger House as though it grew naturally from that very site. The gleaming white fermentation barn, constructed of reclaimed wood using a historic method, appropriately houses the technical aspects of the complex.

8 | Far Niente–

Napa Valley Wine Estate

Nickel Family, owners
Custom Masonry Gravity Flow Winery
Hamben McIntyre, original architects
Ron Nunn, restoration architect

Left: Wine caves were planned but never realized in the late nineteenth century at Far Niente winery. The sixty-foot cave, excavated in 1980 by the late Gil Nickel, became the first in a century in North America. This is the underground wine library located inside the vast network of caves that now exists. The sanctity of the architecture speaks to the reverence with which the wine-making process is administered.

Right: The stone foundation on this carriage house is reminiscent of early European barns with its façade of random stone and two wooden doors framed in stone, capped by a keystone. These doors lead to a storage area that houses a museum for vintage cars.

More than a century old, this weathered stone building called Far Niente is an expression of enduring elegance. Evidence of a stone archway in the cellar suggests that caves were planned here in the nineteenth century, but the death of founder John Benson as well as the era of Prohibition shut the winery down, and it sat empty for a number of years.

Occupying the grounds at Far Niente is this historic stone winery coupled with a large European-style barn, which has a stone foundation, weathered wood siding, and verdigris copper roofing. Pavilions located in various areas around the

Above: Far Niente, originally designed by the architectural firm Hamben McIntyre, is listed as one of the first wineries in Northern California. The beautiful stonework was restored in 1979 by stonemasons who repaired the façade so carefully it has been placed on the National Register of Historic Places.

Right: Gardens are an integral part of Far Niente. In a courtyard near the building stands a stone wishing well articulated in bas-relief.

site, near ponds and flowerbeds, draw visitors into the gardens to enjoy a peaceful wine tasting. The main stone building is an architectural shrine. It was carefully restored and expanded between 1979 and 1982 by stonemasons who rebuilt the old structure so painstakingly exact that it is now listed on the National Register of Historic Places. But some things man cannot improve upon. Over the hundred-year period since Far Niente was built, the finger of nature placed a patina on the stone façade that cannot be reproduced in quite the same way. A mantle of ivy and vines garnish the exterior and embellish the building in a meretricious pattern of greenery. In contrast to the stone, the weathered copper flashing that trims the complicated roofline has aged to a natural verdigris.

When the late Gil Nickel purchased the winery in 1979, one of the first things on the agenda was to revive the idea of building a wine cave near the original stone arch location. Ironically the minimal sixty-square-foot room, dug out of the hillside and connected to the foundation of the building, was the first in a century in the Napa Valley. Fermentation in the cool temperatures of caves set a precedent for the wine industry in Northern California. Today Far Niente has 40,000 square feet of cave corridors storing hundreds of oak barrels for aging wine underground. A secret chamber

Far Niente winery reflected in the pond is a metaphor for the history of the building. The gracious facility is one of the oldest structures in Napa Valley and reverberates today as reflective of the history it carries forward.

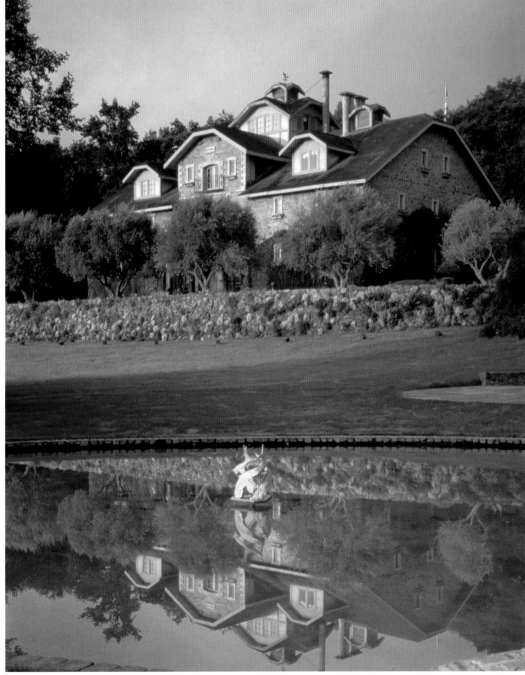

Photo courtesy of Far Niente

Left: This rare wooden spiral staircase is more than a century old and greets visitors in the great hall at the Far Niente winery.

Right: The gardens at Far Niente are often thought of as Southern style. Thirteen acres of grounds surround the main building where the late Gil Nickel began developing the gardens in 1982. The gardens are home to a variety of trees including Japanese maple, snowbell, lion's head maple, and weeping willow.

Far right: Eight thousand azaleas bloom on the grounds at Far Niente and are thought to be the largest planting in California. The blooms and color are visible from nearly a mile away.

Photo by Mary Whitesides

Photo courtesy of Far Niente

Photo courtesy of Far Niente

hidden in one of these corridors is actually a library for storing and tasting distinguished wines from vintage years.

The tasting library is constructed of a framework of ribs called a fan vault, which radiates from stone columns and rises from a polygonal structure. A cluster of grapes and leaves carved from limestone, referred to as a boss, is placed at the apex of the ribbed vault. Positioned in a lit alcove, the stone sculpture of a bearded man holds a cask with great reverence. Tasting wine in this cathedral-like room is an experience reserved for the best vintage years.

Wine tasting and hospitality functions are not the only points of interest on the grounds of Far Niente. The elongated rectangular barn located behind the main building houses a museum of vintage automobiles. The barn, built of all-natural building materials such as stone, wood, and copper, is weathered with brushstrokes from the sun, wind, and rain. Built in the 1990s, it is home to the late Gil Nickel's extensive collection of restored cars. Cordoned off with rope, the antique vehicles are displayed as they would be in a museum. Mr. Nickel's passion for collecting cars adds a surprising dimension to guest tours on the grounds, which are carefully planned and landscaped. The main entrance at the narrow end of the rectangular barn opens from wall to wall, exposing

Photo by Mary Whitesides

a polished concrete floor where the automobiles are parked like modern-day steeds aligned in their stalls. On the broad side of the barn, a side entrance is approached along a vertical stone wall known as a dromos. Heavy timber doors lead to a storage area typically used in vintage barns of this type for keeping hay and feed.

Rooted in the nineteenth century, the Far Niente winery welcomes twenty-first-century guests to its refurbished doors. Whatever the romantic notion is that holds our imagination regarding historic architecture, the age-old Far Niente winery is a reminder of a century in Napa Valley we can only dream of. The strength of such a structure gives credence to the idea that the preservation of noteworthy architecture adds substance to a community, giving future generations the privilege to respect and admire.

Far left: Ivy grows easily in the Northern California climate. Here ivy looks as though it held to the building throughout its hundred-year history. But, because of renovation that took place twenty years ago, it is relatively new.

Left: An underground storage facility leads to 40,000 square feet of caves. Wine barrels will be transferred from here to the caves that maintain a temperature of 58 to 60 degrees with natural humidity levels and a low evaporation rate.

Right: This nearby carriage house on the grounds of Far Niente now houses motorized vehicles. A collection of vintage automobiles is parked on either side of a grand room. The board-and-batten exterior is weather-aged and trimmed in verdigris copper also aged naturally over time.

Viansa
Winery

Tuscan Villa

BAR Architects

Howard J. Backen,
principal architect in charge

The Sebastiani family has constructed a winery analogous to the open markets of Europe. With wine-making roots deeply ensconced in Italy, the Sebastianis have carried on that tradition for generations. Located on a wetland preserve at the southern end of Sonoma County, California, the Viansa Winery has a design that was heavily influenced by the architecture of a Tuscan convent that Sam and Vickie Sebastiani noticed while on vacation. The winery is now a family estate in the wine country where the Sebastianis enthusiastically share their Italian wine-making heritage and authentic Tuscan villa with the public.

The project was realized through the imaginative design work of Howard Backen, principal architect in charge, while at BAR Architects. A spacious piazza

Left: An oak barrel carved with a grape cluster at Viansa Winery is typical of Italian wineries. Oak traditionally interacts with aging wine giving it a desired flavor.

Right: The Sebastianis fell in love with a Tuscan convent while on vacation in Italy. Today their family winery, designed by architect Howard J. Backen while at BAR Architects, is an authentic translation of a Tuscan villa. The large piazza with a fountain and large iron gates is typical of Italian architecture.

welcomes the Viansa guest with all the propriety and drama found at a marketplace in Tuscany. The genteel sound of water musically trickles down a statuette found at the center of old brick pavers where a ring of bistro tables is located. The concept of the arts, good food, and a glass of wine is spread throughout the grounds surrounding the building, where smaller piazzas and more seating can be found. The metal arts are represented as a masterpiece of verdigris vines growing along balustrades. These same vines are articulated on tremendous iron gates located behind the fountain, which lead to the wine caves.

The wine caves have all the charm and color of a historic European counterpart. Oak casks are elevated on stands for fermentation inside the caves and lined up against old plastered walls, creating a strong central axis. Artfully carved antique oak barrels dated 1846 are also on display in a sectioned area of the caves. A small tasting nook adjacent to the cave entrance has the appearance of a farmer's toolshed where wooden rakes and gathering baskets hang from ivy-trimmed walls. Tour groups can get a taste of wine in the shed and enjoy it at the piazza tables before a stroll up semicircular staircases that flank either side of the building.

The second floor houses the Viansa market. An unerring presentation of food, wine, and household treasures is found at this authentic marketplace, similar to

Left, top: The genteel sound of water musically trickles down a statuette found at the center of the piazza located in front of massive iron gates. The gates are beautifully articulated in a vine pattern. Bistro tables where visitors can enjoy a glass of wine can be found around the piazza.

Left, bottom: Antique ceramic jugs on the grounds at Viansa Winery are part of the spirit of the Tuscan environment.

Right: The complexion of the caves at Viansa is decidedly European. The authentic wooden wine casks and double-arched doors are very much like the wine cellars found in the Tuscan countryside.

the ancient concept found in European countries. In the fifteenth century, shopping took place twice a day because refrigeration was not known then. As a result, the freshest ingredients found their way to the table from these markets. The concept of a conglomerate of merchants under one roof provided the opportunity for medieval cities to grow. Common fare found in these markets expresses a broad range of choices; olives, breads, herbs, roast chicken, pates, cheeses, and dressings were presented next to household items along with a vast selection of the finest wines. Food and fine wine, eaten and imbibed in the celebration of art and special affairs, is a ceremonial combination practiced over hundreds of years. The Viansa carries on this tradition with an abundant inventory of wines, sauces, foodstuffs, and gift items.

Photo by Doug Dun / BAR Architects

Left: The ivy-covered walls in a toolshed structure are actually an atmospheric rendition of a farmer's storage space. A glass of wine can be ordered here and visitors can imbibe either inside the shed or on the piazza at any number of bistro tables.

Right: An antique wooden grape press is on exhibit in the wine cellar at the Viansa Winery.

Far right: Multilevel rooflines articulate the multipurpose layout of the Viansa facility and speak to the way it sits on the site. The winery has several entries all accessed on grade. Not only does the building function as a hospitality center, but also as an authentic Italian marketplace where gourmet food and gifts can be found.

Architect Howard Backen has captured the invigorating atmosphere of the Italian open marketplace through his artistic composition of similar elements and materials. The finishes, forms, and configuration of the building's spaces are true to Italian materials and craftsmanship. The flooring is made up of a five-color mix of three-by-five-inch terra-cotta pavers, sized to suit the standard of outdoor pavers found in ancient markets. Laid in a herringbone pattern through the central portion of the Viansa market, a circumference of parallel bricks lead to a deli counter framed by a strip of marble wall. The lighting, off-white tiled walls behind the counter, and a fresco painting leave a sense of wondering whether or not one is actually in Italy. But most striking is the plaster façade on the villa-style facility.

Backen, who is a progenitor of achievement in the authentic appearance of finishes and details, contracted craftsmen to use a three-coat plaster method on the entire skin of the building. The first layer of plaster is a cement color, the second a burnt red, and the third an ocher yellow.

Photo by Doug Dun / BAR Architects

Left: The market occupies the upper level of the building; one can purchase foodstuffs, gifts, and, of course, a bottle of wine. The space is set up much the way markets were in the fifteenth century. The most telling detail is the herringbone-patterned brick pavers found in ancient markets in Europe.

Right: A library of wine choices is available at Viansa Winery, which makes wine from specific species of grapes that guarantee the special flavors they call their own.

The application of the mixture is done in a way that allows the layer below to read through, giving the final product a depth far beyond a flat one-color method. A mass of barrel tiles covers the undulating roofline and binds the building to the sky, which appears as if a painter had interpreted it.

Clearly BAR Architects and Howard Backen have captured the Sebastiani family heritage at the Viansa Winery. Backen acted as intermediary between the family and its strong Italian roots. His imaginative design work and elemental composition of materials has resulted in a Sonoma Valley landmark that carries on a family tradition of wine making, excellent gourmet foodstuffs, and a delicatessen service for which the California wine country can be proud.

10

Stephens House

French Farmhouse
Walker Moody Architects
Sandy Walker, principal architect in charge
Patricia Stephens, interior designer

Left: Architect Sandy Walker of Walker Moody Architects designed the Stephens House around the concept of a French country home. These houses were typically composed as a series of buildings connected by a breezeway. Here, the breezeway is enclosed by an arched ceiling and embellished with spectacular iron gates.

Right: The patchwork effect of French country houses was a result of "add-ons." The French farmers added on to their homes as the need arose and prosperity allowed. This home is a sophisticated interpretation of the same concept.

magine hiking through the hills around Napa Valley and stumbling upon a seventeenth-century French farmhouse rising out of the wooded countryside. Architect Sandy Walker invested the design of the Stephens house with just that kind of patchwork look so typical of old French country houses. French farmers and vineyard owners, or vignerons, were notorious for expanding their homes with add-ons. Indigenous building materials were limited in the French countryside so builders and masons relied on what was available at the time; consequently, the addition did not always match the original structures, and the result was a rambling, or patchwork, effect. The Stephenses, along with their architect Sandy Walker, found inspiration in these homes of the French countryside

WINE COUNTRY | 99

Photo by Mary Whitesides

Above: Interior designer Patricia Stephens imported most of the furnishings in the house. This cabriole leg table and set of web back chairs are rare pieces from Europe.

Right: The antique Spanish pillar in this room is part of a weight-bearing structure. The column was cut in half to enclose the metal, and then the wood refinished to conceal the seam. The wine bar is conveniently located just off the breezeway between the formal dining room and the living room.

and sought to create a similar mood for their dream home.

The design of the home shares many other attributes found in the French country farmhouses. For instance, visitors arriving at the house are led through a formal entry garden to an iron-gated breezeway. The breezeway, a common characteristic of historic French country homes, provided access to carriages as they pulled up to the house. The Stephenses used this romantic notion to serve as an entryway into their home. By enclosing chiseled limestone walls with an arched ceiling, they created a breezeway that connects two separate buildings and makes up the patchwork look of the residence. From here there is an easy entry to the major public and private areas composed as a string of sun-splashed rooms filled with European antiques.

The building on the left includes the great room, library, and master bedroom. The great room readily fulfills the promise of its name with the repose of classical old world symmetry. Glazed on two sides and with ceilings twice as high as the conventional American living room, it immediately lifts the spirits with light and a feeling of space. A richly paneled library adjoins the living room with no connecting hallway.

It is accessed through two giant black-walnut doors; its dark-stained oak paneling has been distressed four times to achieve the desired patina. The owners, interior designer Patricia Stephens and her husband, not only wanted this kind of authentic look for the library but also made sure everything was original. Patricia used a reclaimer to find old beams from a razed French chateau, as well as seven-inch, bow-tie plank flooring which was used in the library and master bedroom. (Bow-tie joiners are an old method of wood inlay used to keep the boards together.) Even the fireplaces, with the exception of the one in the living room, were imported from France. While the smaller fireplaces are fairly common, it is rare to find a larger one, as they must be reclaimed from private estates. The living room fireplace is designed by Street Gardens in New York

Photo by Mary Whitesides

Left: A French country bedroom creates a large private space that can be used for reading, lounging after a bath, or writing a letter at the French writing desk. The headboard is imported from France.

Right: The master bath is situated off a private courtyard where nature can be enjoyed during a soak in the Jacuzzi tub. Soft light enters the room through a vaulted skylight. Towels and bath accessories are in easy reach of the tub.

Photo by Mary Whitesides

and carved in Italy. An old Spanish column marks the corner of the bar in the living room opposite the fireplace. Because this column also bears a structural load, it was split and wrapped around a structural steel member. To even out the irregularities of the split, the wood was bleached. Near the pillar, an arched door leads across the breezeway to the dining room and kitchen.

The building on the right includes the dining room and the kitchen. The finishes here are marked by the hands of time and are paired with the elegance of marble, fine woods, and excellent craftsmanship. Abrecia Vendome marble on the kitchen counters has a soft veneer that stains easily. Through a method called rodding, holes are actually drilled into the underside of the marble and metal rods inserted to harden the surface and prevent stains. The process also makes the marble appear old. The cabinets are crafted of rare white oak glazed in a muted honey color; they go perfectly with the tones of the marble counters. The French chateau floor pattern is made up of pillow-cut limestone framed in wood. In fact, pillow-cut limestone is the standard flooring throughout the house. The timeworn look of old stone coming through ocher-colored plaster in the dining room provides a quietly dramatic effect. Culturally sensitive to the period of the architecture, the authentic furnishings add to the old world aesthetic.

The outdoor living spaces become an expansion of the interior by any number of pocket doors that open to the patios. These spaces have been set up in a series of seating areas on the patios, depending on what kind

Left: Purchased and imported from France, these kinds of stone fireplaces are difficult to find. Many of them are on a small scale; the large ones come from big estates. The beauty of the work and the patina of the finish cannot be duplicated and are achieved only by the march of time.

Right: The Stephens wanted their house to look like an old French farmhouse rising from the landscape. The patchwork effect is typical of the old homes in the French countryside. Horse-drawn carriages were driven through the breezeway to access the house.

Far right: The grounds at Stephens House are broken into a series of spaces used for different purposes. The arbor near the house was inspired by a trip to Portofino, Italy. The sheltered pavilion promotes intimate conversation at a dinner party. An informal gathering can be set at any number of small round tables around the pool. The family maintains a private space near the house just for their own use.

Photo by Mary Whitesides

of entertaining the owners are doing. The pavilion, a concept inspired by a similar facility at the Hotel Splendido in Portofino, Italy, is especially well suited for intimate dinner parties. Several reflective spots, where privacy is respected, are located on the grounds.

Unique contours of the property dictate the nature of the terraced landscape in the rear of the house where all of the plants in the gardens have been methodically adapted to complement the interior color scheme. Orange trees and a profusion of lavenders and yellows reflect the tonal mood of the interiors.

Stephens House well suits its site in the woods of Napa Valley and exudes a historical character found in the architecture of the French farmhouse. Patricia Stephens as owner and interior designer understood the essence of the living spaces so well as to provide the very heart of the home. Architect Sandy Walker's sensitive interpretation of his clients' dream home, his bold integration of vintage architectural elements, and his creative design sense scrupulously helped maintain the family's personal taste. That French farmhouse in the trees that looks as though it has always been there was carefully orchestrated by the designer and the architect.

Franciscan
Oakville Estate

Spanish Mission

BCV Architects:
Hans Baldauf, Ken Calton,
Chris Von Eckartsberg, principals;

Chris Von Eckartsberg, principal
architect in charge;

John Rojas, project manager

Left: Club rooms at the Franciscan Oakville Estate are configured and furnished much like a private den would be. This gives the Franciscan an option to present their finest wines in a personal way. The rooms are located near the gardens and the beauty of the grounds can be seen through large windows.

Right: Gardens measured the prosperity of an estate owner during the Spanish Mission period. The gardens at Franciscan Oakville Estate play off this tradition. Potted plants and courtyards are an integral part of the grounds and the design of the winery.

The Spanish missionaries who settled in California in the eighteenth century brought with them the timeless architectural styles of their homeland. Because the landscape and climate of California was reminiscent of their origins, they were able to establish and build the old world Spanish missions they were accustomed to with little change to original details. The Franciscan Oakville Estate, located along Highway 29 in Oakville, California, pays a contemporary homage to the establishment of these historical missions both in concept and detail. BCV Architects was the chosen firm to update the

Photo by Mary Whitesides

existing facility originally designed in the early 1970s by Architect Wayne Leong.

Typically, the number and kind of details found as part of this type of architecture determined the relative wealth of the mission; the use of a fountain in a center court and the number of gardens and courtyards planned and maintained spoke immediately of affluence. Architects Hans Baldauf, Ken Calton, and Chris Von Eckartsberg, principals of BCV Architects, were influenced by these notions as they set out to reestablish the Franciscan Oakville Estate as a modern-day mission that cultivates and shares the winemaking process with its visiting public.

As one enters the estate from Highway 29, the approach to the buildings is along a central axis where a monumental two-tiered lotus-shaped fountain provides an immutable sense of arrival. Numerous gardens, lush lawns, and towering trees set a bucolic mood.

Just beyond the fountain and the gardens is a small campus of symmetrical buildings tied together by a modern-day tiled roof and prominent clerestory light monitor. BCV took a contemporary approach to the roofing material, substituting the standard Spanish terra-cotta tiles with a galvalum standing seam metal roof applied in a traditional tiled pattern. The exterior integral color plaster is completed with precast-concrete caps laid with a precise joint pattern. At the end of the entry axis is a formal courtyard, which governs the central building's flow of traffic, leading visitors into the grand tasting room. Zinc-topped counters emphasize the formal feel of the room, which is articulated by dark-stained Alaskan white cedar. A high-pitched cedar-lined ceiling is held by a series of impressive trusses. The prominent clerestory windows filter natural light into the room, constantly changing the light quality throughout the day.

The formal atmosphere in the grand tasting room segues into a library cataloged with 10,000

Above: Some visitors who have entered through the grand tasting hall have the option to be escorted to the library where a vast array of wines is on display. Franciscan Oakville Estate catalogs 10,000 bottles of wine here.

Right: A simple hallway connects the private club rooms with the library at the Franciscan. Textured gray walls contrast the charcoal color of the finished floor tiles and a simple bouquet of flowers adds just enough texture to otherwise basic tones and finishes.

bottles of wine where one can enjoy a formal tasting seated at a long communal table. The library has a closed roof to maintain a rich dark feeling—a metaphor for the dark rich wines. Smaller private tasting rooms found in connecting alcoves allow the visitor to sample the product of individual wineries also a part of the Franciscan Oakville Estate. The layered complexity in this building leads to the ultimate personal

Left: A large fountain became the symbolism of success according to the philosophy of Spanish Mission architecture. This gigantic fountain in the middle of the roundabout is a thrilling entrance to the main tasting room at the Franciscan.

Below, left: Bracketed shed roofs protect the windows of the Franciscan from the heat and glare of the sun. Rain is directed away from the building by the sloped shape.

Below, right: The chimneys are a calculated design feature at the Franciscan. Not only are they functional, but they also add a beautiful silhouette to the roofline.

experience. Located in a private corridor on the windowed side of the building are intimate club-rooms furnished much like a living room in a private home. Leather-upholstered chairs dressed with side tables and lamps provide the comfort of an easy chair in which to enjoy a glass of fine wine.

The Franciscan Oakville Estate has a philosophy: "The wines are the elegant expression of the vineyards, giving unique voice to the terroir on which they are grown." *Terroir* is defined as an inclusive combination of soil, topography, and microclimate. The expression of the architecture adheres to this philosophy as BCV Architects reworked the existing facility to fit comfortably into the vineyard setting. The winery now has a definite identity that communicates the fact that it is a distinctive structure in the Napa Valley. While maintaining a contemporary viewpoint for contemporary needs, the Franciscan Oakville Estate endorses the Spanish Mission architectural heritage of the eighteenth-century monks who settled this area with grace and dignity.

12

Walker House

Contemporary
Walker Moody Architects
Sandy Walker, architect

Left: The private entrance found in the rear gardens at the Walker House showcases the entire double story common area. The windows frame a dramatic circular staircase that provides access to two bedrooms, a home office, and a sitting area.

Right: A strategically placed table and chairs provide an area for adults to monitor the activities of children who enjoy either the pool or the nearby tennis court. Sheltered by an arbor covered with vines, adults remain cool during their vigil. This is one of many outdoor options at this weekend retreat.

A weekend retreat located down a country lane in Napa Valley is tucked so skillfully into the landscape that one could pass it by quite easily. Although just off the road a few hundred yards, it has a sense of complete privacy. The house is oriented on the site so as to expose the narrowest face to the road and the broadest façade to nature. Simple in form with moderate square footage, the charm of this house unfolds one layer at a time.

A small courtyard hidden behind a wooden gate provides a sense of arrival. One is immediately taken by the sophistication and cool simplicity of the house. A blanket of ivy softens the straightforward stucco exterior and a second-story balcony interrupts the plain wall surface with a curved balustrade. The garage, which is adjacent to the house, does not interfere with the architecture. A windowed front door invites the eye to enter the house first.

A step inside reveals a wondrous volume of space where ceilings rise more than twenty feet, and the entrance, living room, and dining room open to a view of the garden through a wall of windows. Lawn, flowers, and trees have a symbiotic relationship with the rooms inside. The eye catches the edge of an outdoor pergola christened with wisteria, which disappears down a corridor to a quiet sitting area.

This contemporary retreat mixes indoor and outdoor spaces with an ambition that never sacrifices refinement or relaxation. Massive shade trees

Below: Although this looks like a formal living room, it is actually considered an outdoor room. The wicker furniture is made plush by overstuffed cushions. The space is opened on one end and exposed to nature where a view of the pool is close at hand. Lowering a metal roll-up door can lock in the space making it secure during the workweek.

Right: A heavy glass-topped coffee table on industrial wheels is easily moved to accommodate the need. The wheels add a funky design element to the table. A view of the track for the metal roll-up door can be seen here.

Left: A buoyant, open, and airy circular staircase bends gracefully from the main floor to two bedrooms on the second floor. An otherwise angular room gains interest with these fluid lines. Not only does the staircase contribute to the beauty of the architecture but it is also an efficient use of space.

Right: Contemporary art is hung throughout the house and arranged in groupings on the walls. Three-dimensional art like this series of "white colors" lends an air of humor to the house.

dissolve the outdoor light that would otherwise be harsh. There is a harmony of subtle design decisions at play in this house, which challenge one's senses without assaulting them. White walls and concrete floors provide a Zen-like atmosphere where a white spiral staircase appears to ascend to infinity.

Layers of outdoor spaces emanate from the house like rings in a ruffled pond. Large glass doors off the dining area lead to a collage of wicker sofas embraced by three walls and open to nature on one side. A cascade of jasmine surrounds a sculptural table overhung by a sensuous painting. This sheltered gallery is a convenient vantage point from which to watch children playing in the swimming pool. A roll-up metal door secures the outdoor room when the house is locked.

Venturing further into nature, another

Photo by Mary Whitesides

outdoor room with a table set for Sunday brunch is wrapped in trees and complemented by the sky. Across the way, stools await someone who might order a glass of chardonnay at a bar backed by a weathered fence. In a seating area under the umbrella of a catalpa tree, one can find seclusion to enjoy the Sunday paper.

Whereas kitchens these days are designed as gathering spaces themselves, the utilitarian one in this house has been designed to service several entertainment areas throughout the house. Preparing a meal is accomplished effortlessly. The

Photo by Mary Whitesides

Furniture in a contemporary home can be uninviting. But not so in this one. The curved leather barrel chairs invite one to be embraced by comfort. The fireplace has no surround. The clean lines are repeated in a duplicate shape where wood is stored.

appliances, cupboards, and pantry are within steps of the central island.

One of the main gathering places is the media room. A group of avid sports fans can hobnob for an afternoon football game in a more personal space with lower ceilings and one narrow doorway. Soft light shimmers through UV-protective window shades, adding warmth to a spirited gathering.

The true genius of this weekend retreat is its manageable size which requires minimal upkeep. Art and sculpture adorn the interiors so naturally, it gives the house a gallery-like feel without becoming overly formal. Paradoxically the house remains thoroughly child-friendly, and guests feel comfortable putting their feet up on the coffee table.

Architect Sandy Walker has created an elegant design for a weekend retreat that welcomes its visitors with a progression of indoor and outdoor spaces. The two exist in a symbiotic relationship that begins to express the nature in which it is experienced. However, the true lyricism of the architecture is caught in the luminescent glow of sunset, when the house is lit and calls the soul indoors for renewal.

13 | Classic Modern House

BAR Architects: Architecture
Richard Beard, principal
Ken Linsteadt, project architect
Babey Moulton Jue and Booth: Interior Design
Michael Booth, principal

Vicky Doubleday: Interior Design

While many houses throughout the wine country are inspired by historic European architecture and interiors, this home was inspired by contemporary European design. The placement, shapes, and numbers of furnishings are carefully calculated to be adequate without cluttering.

According to architect Richard Beard of BAR Architects, numerous residents moving into the wine country share a vision of creating simple yet elegant architectural styles for living. Many of his clients have the desire to stay away from traditional styles and are looking instead at exploring more contemporary expressions in their homes. The clients for this particular house wrote Beard an essay about the kind of life they live, how they wished to use the house to serve their needs, how their philosophy about nature should interact with the house, and practical issues that needed to be considered.

The site was a challenging combination of valley converging along a mountainous terrain. The client wanted the house to be touched by nature but not intimidated by it. The challenge then, was in the given context—to create a shelter that would protect its inhabitants from the elements outdoors yet not exclude the outdoors from its inhabitants. The solution was to design a structure that had a symbiotic relationship with its surroundings; to do this Beard created a unique design consisting of two interlocking structures that embrace a series of courtyards. The dual structure idea provided a means by which Beard could orient the main building toward Dry Creek Valley and still have part of the house oriented toward the more rugged and pristine wild landscape

Photo by Doug Dun / BAR Architects

to the southwest. The two separate viewpoints created an opportunity to differentiate sections of the house as to usage, interplay of light, and privacy.

Trees, mountains, and valleys contribute the environmental context whereby the approach up the driveway reveals the house slowly. Foliage gives way to the understated house, which has a quiet, meditative quality contributing to a Zen-like feeling. The clean, uncluttered surface is a combination of concrete and stucco. The structural form is classic with two rigid rectangular shapes that share matching hip roofs. An organic overlay tempers the architecture with randomly placed native plants.

Passive environmental design elements direct natural daylight into the

Photo by Doug Dun / BAR Architects

house. Broad shed roofs protect a lineup of French doors against accumulating sunlight, making heat transfer minimal. Windows are oriented to catch ambient light rather than direct sunbeams. Radiant mornings are cheerful, not blaring; evenings are rosy, not intrusive. The window placement also acts as an elemental ventilation system. Wind patterns directed through the house cool without attracting gusts that slam doors.

The understated approach to the house is enlivened by comfortable warm colors and open airy rooms. People become the highlight of the space as the house provides a backdrop for their interactions. Simple, square rooms are an invitation to let go the required attention of an overly designed interior. The choice of interior materials, including a plain-surface plaster-veneer fireplace, smooth-finished plaster walls, and concrete floors, are punctilious background elements for red trimmed rugs, ribbed ceilings, and rich wooden cabinets. American cherry wood floors in the hallway are an ebullient material providing a warm contrast to the concrete floors.

It is easily noted that this house has a contemporary European influence. The architecture is clean, efficient, and contemporary. This influence is most notable in the kitchen. Entertaining is an important aspect of life for this family and their kitchen is a key ingredient in making that happen. The layout is segregated in to workstations, allowing the cook to prepare meals and entertain guests at the same time. Architect Richard Beard describes the kitchen as "a room you walk into that happens to be a kitchen." Showy appliances are absent in place of functional ones,

Photo by Tim Street Porter

Left: The bathroom in the guest-house is simple, clean, and uncluttered. Every amenity needed in the bathroom can be stored in this shelved table—a counter without cabinet doors or too many drawers.

Right: Three small rugs placed on the floor complete a pattern as though one rug. Simplicity is not easily achieved. Anything out of place becomes blatantly apparent. Every item in this hall is placed according to shape, color, scale, and balance.

Left: Efficiency of space, carefully placed furniture, and an art-lamp contribute to a space that is contemporary in look and inviting in comfort. The soft texture of the upholstery fabrics contrasts with the virginal white walls.

Right: A lap pool located on a concrete platform overlooking an incredible landscape brings nature to this home without allowing it to intrude on the living space.

Photo by Tim Street Porter

and the space is navigated as effortlessly as would be found in a modern European kitchen.

In addition to the kitchen, another important room for entertaining is the billiard room, carefully situated in a smaller semi-separate building where windows catch the changing light, altering the character of the space. The room is a special space where the boys in the family can hang out with their father and play a game.

The European-born owner of this house has a sophisticated

Photo by Doug Dun / BAR Architects

eye for furniture pieces and accessories. He and interior designer Michael Booth worked together to come up with a mix of antique, classic, and modern furniture, with choices based on simple shape and form. The placement of pieces is carefully considered on the basis of how these forms work together when placed in a configuration. Although the look of the house is meant to be minimal, it is in a state of flux as pieces are added and subtracted from the interiors. Both owner and designer are always mindful of the fine line between clutter and austerity.

This home exemplifies an originally designed shelter that suits a family like a finely tailored garment. The clients took the time to analyze their needs and wishes in writing. Comprehensive communication between client and architect will ensure the homeowner a highly personalized piece of architecture that functions efficiently for individual needs. Architect Richard Beard of BAR Architects answered the issues here with sensitivity and finesse.

14

Mumm Napa Valley Winery

Traditional Rutherford Barn
BAR Architects:
Richard Beard and Bob Arrigoni,
principals in charge

Mumm Napa Valley Winery is partially hidden by ancient oak trees preserved during the construction process. Because it is located on the Silverado Trail, the structure was designed to be low-key and visually noninvasive. Wildflowers grow in a pattern of their own, a natural contribution to the building.

Mumm is a no-nonsense winery for the people and visitors of the Napa Valley. Skillfully designed by BAR Architects Richard Beard and Bob Arrigoni, the facility takes on the classic all-American barn vernacular with an industrial flare. The hospitality is down-home friendly and the staff members at the winery are casually dressed in jeans, just as they would be if they were Mumm family members working on the family farm.

Sited at the base of a knoll off the Silverado Trail in Rutherford, California, Mumm is partially hidden by ancient oak trees preserved during the construction process. Because it is located on a main road, the owners wanted the structure to be low-key and as visually noninvasive as an early Northern California farmer's barn. The large building slotted between the oak grove and

Photo by Doug Dun / BAR Architects

the vineyards synthesizes so successfully with the background that passersby see only a hint of it. Like the face of a weathered farmer, the wood siding has been left without a finish so it may age naturally over time as it is exposed to the elements. The board-and-batten facing is the same choice as that of the early farmers in the area, who took great pride in their barn buildings. An entrance corridor, which leads to a courtyard of groomed gardens, is hugged by the architecture.

The schematic layout of the building is exposed inside the courtyard. Rectangular forms are arranged in an L-shaped complex where the courtyard, hallway, gift shop, and magnanimous hospitality room accommodate touring visitors. Generous hallways with vast lengthy walls direct the flow of traffic to various destinations within the building and serve as an exhibition space. Down-to-earth displays of the works of historic photographers such as Ansel Adams strike the same organic response as does the winery facility. A country gift shop is stocked

Photo by Doug Dun / BAR Architects

with homey jams, baskets, wines, and logo items. Hospitality functions where a visitor can taste wine and enjoy the vineyards are held in an unusually light-filled space. A sophisticated version of a glass-enclosed room, added onto the exterior like a shed, gives the wine tasters telescopic views into the open vineyards. Here, sipping a glass of the final product comes full circle.

BAR Architects has captured the all-American barn with the same sensitive pride as the early farmers' barns of Rutherford. The architecture carries on the agricultural legacy that bespeaks the philosophy of the winery, unobstructed by formality or ceremony. At Mumm Napa Valley Winery, what is presented is what you experience.

Below, left: Vineyards located in front of the Mumm winery help ground the building to nature and communicate the intent that this is indeed a farming industry.

Below, right: Bold metal straps on rich wooden doors are not only functional hinges but also strong design elements in this simple atmosphere.

Right: Visitors are comfortable in casual attire at the Mumm winery where employees dress informally as well.

Photo by Doug Dun / BAR Architects

15

Doilney House

Vintage Cottage
St. Helena, California

Left: This vintage cottage located in St. Helena, California, is thought to be more than a hundred years old. The master bedroom is not part of the original structure but was recently added to the house. The grand curved window opens to an unobstructed view of the Berringer vineyard.

Right: The back porch faces toward the vineyards and is connected to the oldest part of the house where the current kitchen is located.

Vintage homes in the wine country region of Northern California are encyclopedias of history. St. Helena is one community filled with a significant number of buildings and homes that are more than a hundred years old. Without a strong sense of preservation amongst the citizens in this town, the age-old traditions would be lost. The agricultural heritage of this fertile region spawned a number of prosperous farmers and tradesmen who expressed that abundance in their homes, which became trademarks for a way of life encompassing good wine, good food, and the arts. Hardly a visitor or homeowner is immune to the charms of St. Helena. The current populace is filled with citizens who passionately protect, maintain, and improve upon this established ambience.

Photo by Mary Whitesides

Photo by Mary Whitesides

Over the years as Mike and Toni Doilney raised their family in Park City, Utah, they dreamed of living in the wine country. Now with their children grown they live that dream. As proprietors of a charming cottage-style home that is thought to be nearly a century and a half old, they now live a life closer to the earth. The fluid sound of York Creek running beside the house is a reminder that this is a country setting. Many old hand-quarried stone bridges, signed and dated by the engineers, may be found scattered throughout the St. Helena area. One near this house is marked 1903. The rambling scheme of the house has been defined through a series of add-ons. Only three families of record have owned the house in more than a century. Each family altered the home with care to fit the individual needs of the inhabitants and the time period within which they lived. The Doilneys found a history book of information in layers of roof, plaster, lath, wallboard, and changes of flooring materials. In the 1870s and 1880s, an Italianate style of architecture became popular in rural California. The center section of this house has a false front, flat roof, bracketed trim, columned entry, and curved doors—all details of this style. Perhaps these are clues that this section was built during the late nineteenth century.

The first owner was born in the original country cottage and lived there for over eighty years before

Left: A charming window seat is located off the oldest section of this vintage cottage at the head of a vast entrance corridor. The house was altered a number of times over the years and contains a history book of information in layers of materials used during each period.

Right: A view of the vineyards from the back porch reminds the Doilney family that they live close to the earth. Gardens grow easily here and the family enjoys not only a culinary garden but also the abundance of the land on a larger scale by growing a vineyard owned together with a group of friends. Their first vintage wine named Maple Lane is now available.

Photo by Mary Whitesides

passing away. The house was remodeled many times in the twentieth century. The second owner, who found the house in a state of disrepair, remodeled and made additions for modernization. When the Doilneys purchased the house in 1999, they added the master bedroom on the foundation of the carport at the rear of the house; this room has an unobstructed view of the vineyard. They also constructed a new garage in place of an old chicken coop that stood on the banks of York Creek.

Below: An eclectic mix of American country antiques, paintings, and folk art represents history, travel, and a love of art. The dining room is a gallery for some of these objects and furnishings.

Right: In the new section of the house a tile floor is distinguished by a path of pebbles laid out in a diamond pattern. The back hallway connects the formal living room with the master suite and provides the option to enter the courtyard or leave the house.

Photo by Mary Whitesides

The entrance to this house is fronted by a yard filled with lush vegetation and guarded by a two- to three-hundred-year-old oak tree, one of St. Helena's many heritage trees. Standing in the entry, one notices the unusual height of the ceilings, which present an unexpected grandeur. The Berringer vineyard hugs the house on two sides and is framed by a large window in the living room. A large portion of the house is visually open from the entry. A long, broad gallery runs nearly the length of the house from the kitchen, past the dining room and living room to the guest bedroom. The house radiates a homey country feeling because of the home furnishings and the interior finishes. The family room that blends into the kitchen is the original one-room structure. Two small bedrooms, a bathroom, garden room, laundry room, and study open off

the family room and kitchen. The kitchen is flowing with genial warmth, with distressed cabinets finished in a French blue and the walls painted an eggshell white, much like a Dresden plate. Oak flooring throughout the house remains true to the period in which the house was first built.

Collections of folk art, quilts, and books add to the country ambience throughout. Toni, who is adept at arranging art and interesting objects in and around the house, ties it all together in a seamless eclectic mix, one that represents history, travel, and their love of art. The first painting purchased in 1968 has grown into a collection ranging from contemporary sculpture and paintings to antique textiles and American folk art.

St. Helena represents the best of rural life, including an enduring natural beauty and the sophistication of a cosmopolitan community nearby. This vintage house has a patina of time and history that has left layers of character that reach out to extend tradition without destroying the core intent—traditions that include agriculture, architecture, fine wine, good food, and the arts. The vintage homes in St. Helena are architectural treasures tended by modern-day citizens who passionately preserve the heritage of the wine country.

16

Staglin Family Estate

Italian Villa with a Palladian Influence
BAR Architects:
Bob Arrigoni, principal architect in charge
John Loomis, SWA Landscape Architects
Trina LaRoche, interior designer
Eff Goodwin, interiors for BAR

Enormous arched doorways and windows funnel light into the Staglin home fulfilling the family's main request for a space large enough to hang their art collection. The lighting, both natural and utilitarian, highlights each individual art piece, which is displayed to its fullest advantage.

f music can be heard coming from the hills of Rutherford, California, the strains may very well be drifting from the Staglin family vineyard. Well known throughout Rutherford, California, for annually sponsoring charitable music festivals, the family has raised $22 million dollars over a nine-year period for mental-health research. Held on the grounds of their estate, the festivals are just one of the ways the family contributes to the legacy of the community. The Palladian-style architecture of the Staglin family compound, meticulously orchestrated by BAR Architects, demonstrates timelessness in design that is a metaphor for the community ideal.

The Staglin family has strong ties to Italy, including its architecture and agriculture. The original family name, Stagliano, was changed after they immigrated to the United States. Their Italian roots include a love of Palladian architecture that both Garen and Shari Staglin share. Because of this, the couple once had a desire to live in Lake Como, Italy. But after practical considerations, they decided to build an Italian country villa in the Napa Valley, where the residence would get more use. Andrea Palladio, a master Italian Renaissance architect, is perhaps the most influential architect in the Western world. His carefully proportioned pediment buildings became models for stately homes and government buildings in Europe and America. Palladio, who studied the classical architecture of the Roman ruins, placed two tenets on his design work: (1) the scheme of the architecture must be symmetrical, and (2) the building must fit within the landscape, not take away from it. Palladio commonly used pillars, arches, and loggia in his architecture; these elements have become a signature of what are called Palladian buildings.

The Staglin family estate is located on sixty-two acres of premium land in the vineyard region of

Photo by Doug Dun / BAR Architects

Left: Entrance to the Staglin home ends in a sizable courtyard designed to handle a number of vehicles. The house is an earthen color that matches the topographical soils called "Rutherford dust."

Right: One of the distinctive features of Palladian architecture is a grand loggia. Palladio and the tenets he set forth in his architecture fascinated the Staglin's. Many features distinguished in his designs are found at their home. This loggia is accessed from several rooms in the house through a symmetrical line of French doors.

Photo by Doug Dun / BAR Architects

Photo by Doug Dun / BAR Architects

Rutherford, California. The property encompasses the Staglin family winery, vineyards, and private residence. BAR Architects designed the private residence to easily fit into the design tenets of Palladio. Bob Arrigoni, architect in charge of the project, is an Italian American with strong ties of his own to Italy. Understanding full well the Palladio edicts, he drew the schematic layout of the Italian country villa as a

Photo by Doug Dun / BAR Architects

series of symmetrical structures arranged asymmetrically to accommodate the steep site. All parts of the house are literally arranged to parallel the slope, with one grand gallery joining the buildings. One of the most appealing details of the villa is the stucco color of the façade, which matches the vineyard soils known as "Rutherford dust." The dwelling appears to grow from the dark, rich earth, fulfilling the first design tenet of Palladio. The organic look of the house does not take away from the land but blends with its environs. Just as the mineral content in soils causes a natural variegation of color, the same superlative idea inspired the designers to choose multicolored barrel tiles for the roof. Eleven different shades are randomly placed, mimicking nature's own discretionary use of color. Color, symmetry, and texture continue to play an important role inside the house too.

Architect Bob Arrigoni used terra-cotta floor tiles on the interior floor

Photo by Doug Dun / BAR Architects

space, extending them through to the outdoor patios and loggia. The tonal qualities of the tile are ideally matched with the tones of the exterior skin. The radiance of the eggshell walls exudes warmth through the depth of carefully crafted smooth-finish plaster walls. Trina LaRoche, interior designer, chose a mix of rich colored fabrics, leathers, and woods that contrast with the glowing walls yet mix well together with compatible undertones.

Perhaps the most compelling detail inside the house is the twenty-two-foot-high wooden-beamed ceiling in the living room, which creates a dramatic effect that adds volume to a standard-size space. Enormous arched doorways and windows funnel light into this and other areas of the house, fulfilling the family's main request for wall space to display an extensive art collection started in 1970. A well-lit extended hallway acts as the art gallery, providing the axiomatic space needed to hang a good portion of the collection.

The exacting symmetry of the house is visible from many viewpoints within the floor plan. A penumbra of doorways and rooms, including dining room, kitchen, coffee room, and family room, can be seen from the living room. Twelve sets of French doors run the length of the house. A broad loggia is accessed through several of these doors where the transition to the outdoors has all the comforts of indoor furnishings and the pleasures of viewing nature.

The grounds and gardens were designed in tandem with the house by landscape architect John Loomis of SWA Landscape Architects, who chose 100 percent organic vegetation and biodiverse systems such as beehives to control bugs. Lavender fields and olive groves were also planted to protect the vineyards from harmful insects. A strategically planned corridor between the stream and the vineyards was planted with radishes, carrots, clover, and vetch to draw destructive insects away from the vineyards.

Included on the grounds are bocce ball courts. Bocce ball, a game that originated in Italy centuries ago, is becoming quite popular again today in the wine country. Perfect for an afternoon social, the game does not require a lot of skill or knowledge. The rules are made up as the game progresses, assuring everyone creative involvement.

Photo by Doug Dun / BAR Architects

The full rounded life of the Staglin family, where business and personal lifestyle colludes with relaxation and nature, easily satisfies the needs of its members. Architect Bob Arrigoni, interior designer Trina LaRoche, and landscape architect John Loomis have all contributed to the Staglin family compound in a way that is congruous with their love of Palladian architecture, the creature comforts of the owners, and the ecological rhythms of the landscape that embraces the compound. A gracious way of life shared by the family with friends and neighbors, where charitable music festivals are held to make an important contribution to a highly important cause, will be found at the Staglin residence.

Photo by Erhard Pfeiffer

17

Napa Valley Residence

Environmental Architecture with an Asian Flair

Backen Gillam Architects:
Howard J. Backen, architect

Jack Chandler, landscape architect

Jacques Saint Dizier, interior designer

The owners of this Napa Valley residence hired architect Howard J. Backen to design a house based on the screened porches they grew up with. Backen essentially ended up designing a screened house. From this viewpoint, nature visibly runs right through the center of the house from hillside to the edge of the pond.

The Palisades, an impressive geologic formation, is the backdrop for an unassuming residence designed by Howard J. Backen. This home, sited on the edge of a pond in the Stags Leap region of the Napa Valley, rests quietly at the base of the Palisades. These mountain peaks reflect and absorb the natural mood of their surroundings at all hours of the day; the sun rises over the peaks at dawn and shines back on them at sunset, creating a brilliant array of purples, pinks, and blues. At moonrise they glow with a hint of white that may be traced to a formal reflection in the pond. Watched from a deck hovering over the shoreline, this natural phenomenon becomes an integral part of everyday life for the owners. The symbiotic relationship between this man-made shelter and its natural surroundings hovers

Photo by Erhard Pfeiffer

Because of a childhood in Southern California where outdoor living was a given, the owner wanted that same kind of access to nature. The master bedroom is linked directly to the pond by a small deck located through pocket doors that disappear into thick walls. A red chair, situated in the perfect position to contemplate the Palisades, accents the basic color scheme.

somewhere between the satisfaction of practical human necessity and a most minimal interruption of nature.

The owners came to architect Howard Backen with the idea of building a small, unobtrusive house slung low on the banks of an acre of pond. What has been created is just that, a house so well camouflaged with the surrounding vegetation that one cannot see it from the road. The house takes its form at gentle angles conforming to the curve of the pond's edge. A sod roof visually blends with the landscape so well that from a viewpoint above the house the structure disappears within the existing shoreline. A ribbon of copper fascia that runs along the entire roofline is a precise delineation connecting the exterior walls and the sod roof. The neutral-toned cut stone chosen for the foundation sets a meditative tonal quality for all the materials used on the house.

The owners, drawn to an outdoor lifestyle, asked Backen for a screened porch. His response was to take this idea one step further, essentially designing a screened house. Sectioned into three parts as a definition for living, the house may be described to have the yin, the yang, and a unifying element. On the approach to the home, one descends from the roofline down a swagger of stone stairs where shoji screen entrance doors are a clue to the Japanese influences throughout the interiors. The prudent simplicity of Japanese houses suits the philosophy of the owners, who chose Asian details for their lucid qualities. One coffered ceiling detail they found pictured in a Japanese home defines the yin section of the house, and is translated into two-by-twelve-foot hemlock planks, simulating the coffered ceiling in the living room, dining room, and kitchen areas. The detailing in the ceiling leads the eye across the house, where the delineation between interior and exterior is noted only by the walls that act as pockets for large sliding glass doors. Beyond the doors, a simple deck reaches six feet out over the water's edge, hovering above the pond as if it were a lily pad.

The bedroom, master bathroom, and library compose the yang section of the house, where again the access to nature is through pocket doors, satisfying the owners' desire to create an indoor/outdoor living experience familiar to them from living in Southern California. In the library, a skylight is added to funnel light into the only room that does not face the water. The unconventional niches crafted by carpenter Mike Peck display an outstanding collection of ancient Asian figures.

Interior designer Jacques Saint Dizier remained sensitive to the palette established by the neutral exterior colors, natural vegetation, and simplicity of the owners' intent. Sea-grass carpets cover the floors, simulating the wheat-colored hills of the wine country. Upholstery fabrics are without pattern, playing on texture and subtle color tones instead. Leather sofas and plush chairs polarize the yin-yang intent of the architecture. The third section where these two planes meet is a neutral utilitarian ground, housing the garage and home office.

Pocket doors run the length of the house giving access to the pond from all major rooms. The living room is no exception and while a formal conversation may be going on around the coffee table, the sounds of nature can be heard. Interior designer Jacques Saint Dizier remained sensitive to the color palette established by the natural vegetation.

This home is a well-articulated piece of architecture that functions efficiently on a utilitarian level. The ceilings are held low, never exceeding nine feet six inches, a calculated choice to manage the scale of the house in relation to the pond. Heat gain is easily managed because of the ceiling height and the insulation provided by the sod roof, eliminating the need for mechanical air-conditioning. In winter, the heat absorbed by the roof throughout the day augments the radiant-floor coils, easily maintaining a natural comfort level.

Photo by Erhard Pfeiffer

During the hot summers, open doors allow breezes to flow through the house night and day, again blurring the lines between indoors and out.

A garden of indigenous grasses envelops the house and joins the countryside as though it had never been touched. Jack Chandler, landscape architect, often composes his work as an improvisation on nature. He has added accents of old

Photo by J. D. Peterson

Japanese maples, bamboo, and butterfly iris. Visitors arriving at the house in the spring are welcomed by a roof garden blooming with wildflowers such as golden poppies, lupine, vetch, and California fuchsia. In the hot summer months the vegetation turns golden, merging with the hills across the pond.

This home forms a partnership with, rather than an invasion of, nature. Man-made structures that respect natural elements—managing rather than destroying, enhancing instead of replacing, and improving upon rather than diminishing from—express an unspoken peace of mind and wellness between living things. A sense of simplicity and artistic enhancement go hand in hand when the team of players understands the characteristics of nature itself. The balance between the vibrancy of yin and reflective quality of yang achieved in the design of this house manifests the Japanese philosophy preferred by the owners. It is the true definition of retreat: peaceful and full of solitude.

Photo by J. D. Peterson

18

Backen Residence

Napa Valley Farmhouse
Backen Gillam Architects:
Howard J. Backen, architect

Left: This farmhouse-style complex located in the rolling hills of Oakville, California, has a series of buildings strategically oriented to certain views. The open feeling of this arbor near the pool coaxes one to enjoy the outdoors partially sheltered by the open structure, and the outdoor fireplace remedies cool evenings.

Right: Architect Howard J. Backen designed a home to suit the specific needs of his family. Several outbuildings are located around the property according to the activities they serve. The pool house is an area where friends and family can be entertained and the house doubles as a guesthouse.

Located in Oakville, California, where grapevines ribbon the rolling hills of the wine country, is a complex of buildings inspired by traditional farmhouse-style architecture. Not clustered in the conventional manner, the complex is scattered around the property, strategically placed to accommodate different family activities and take advantage of the 360-degree views. The house is eminently suited to its agricultural site, and the vineyards graciously surrender to the hereditary

Photo by J. D. Peterson

Photo by Erhard Pfeiffer

aesthetic of the house and outbuildings. Even though the spirit of the structures is rooted in the agricultural history of the wine country, a progressive sensitivity is evident.

Howard J. Backen, architect, has designed a home for his family that has a sense of timelessness and expresses his architectural passion for rural-style buildings. The lucid, straightforward architecture is filled with inspired spaces that maximize the site, and coaxes one to enjoy the outdoors. A long drive up the hill mingles with the vineyard, settling on an approach to a

board-and-batten house painted saffron yellow. A typical covered porch instantly welcomes and directs the visitor up a series of stairs to the front door of the residence.

An expansive, rectangular barn-like room pulls one into the public domain where kitchen, dining room, and living room stretch from one end to the other. Furniture groupings summon different activities to defined spaces that have no walls. Backen's two-bedroom, two-bathroom home has an ethereal quality that is unexplainably comforting. A rejuvenating energy fills the rooms that is both stimulating and restful. The color of walls, the placement of windows, and the framing of nature all play a part in this. There is vibrancy in the tones of the off-white painted walls and vaulted ceilings, and a purity within the backdrop it provides the inhabitants, the furnishings, and the landscape, which is visible along the entire length of the room. The

Left: Guests staying at the pool house have a magnificent view of the pool and a bevy of trees across the lawn.

Right: The structure of the pool house/guesthouse is simple, open, and clean. The colors blend in a way so that the furnishings are tasteful but do not command attention. People become the focus in a space like this.

Photo by J. D. Peterson

landscape of rolling vineyards is visible because of Backen's signature glass pocket doors that lead to a sweeping eight-foot-wide veranda. The porch is broad enough to hang a hammock and long enough for clustered groupings of wicker furniture with room to spare.

The kitchen, sectioned by a zinc-covered bar surrounded by classic wooden stools, invites conversation with the cook, allowing preparation of a meal to become part of the social milieu. If a guest should wander to the dining area, fireplace, or living room, a convivial atmosphere remains part of one capacious room. Red wicker barrel chairs explode with color around an extended antique dining table overhung by a wrapped wire chandelier. Country-style plank flooring runs the length of the room while carefully placed contemporary sisal rugs help to define gathering spaces.

Perhaps the most compelling accouterment in the house is found in the private realm. Connected to the master bedroom is an outdoor shower located across a secluded slate courtyard. The primitive freedom of an outdoor shower has been accomplished through a carefully planned schematic where the exterior walls of the house and an opposing wall buffer the area, which has no roof. A hot tub, adjacent to the shower, is sunk into the slate flooring and looks out across the grapevines hugging the property.

The master bedroom is filled with overstuffed country sofas placed around a white brick fireplace. One entire wall of the room opens out through large barn doors to the veranda and breathtaking valley views. Backen has created a home that is at peace with nature on several levels, whether it is a veranda that coaxes one out to observe the surroundings, or an outdoor shower semi-sheltered from the elements, or a pool where one can blatantly bask in the sun.

Not far from the main residence is a captivating pool house paralleled by a lap-length pool. The frank open area is an exemplary space for entertaining friends and family with varying possibilities of finding comfort. One can choose a variety of seating arrangements, from lounges around the pool to a covered portico with a fireplace at the pool house. A small kitchen, family room, and bathroom complete the arrangements for the structure to also function as a guest cottage.

Photo by Mark Darley

Left, below: Maximum efficiency in use of space earmarks this one contiguous space in the Backen home. The windows are configured so that the light has an ethereal quality inside the house. The kitchen blends into the dining room and through to the living room.

Right: The view from this window makes guests feel they are looking at a gigantic landscape painting. The pocket windows in the master bedroom open to frame this painting by nature.

A well cared for home with a level of comfort, which is meticulously thought out and properly arranged, exudes an unexplainable essence that adds marrow to a dwelling. When architecture respects the land, its surrounding site features, and its views, it tends to come alive, turning a house into a home, reverberant with the pleasures of the human spirit. Architect Howard Backen designed a home for his family that matches his creative lifestyle. This is a sophisticated home where he can entertain friends in the casual atmosphere of the rolling vineyards that embrace each building, a home that functions with all of the fundamental ingredients to make it hum.

Photo by Erhard Pfeiffer

How to Achieve Wine Country Style

"Architecture is about scale, proportion, texture, color, and attention to detail. All of these things invoke emotional responses in people, whether they know it or not . . . quite honestly there are places people feel more comfortable than others based purely on their scale and proportion, light and texture. People don't know why, it is an innate response that we can later justify."

—JESSIE WHITESIDES, Architect

The architectural spirit of wine country, as varied as it may be, shares several common attributes: A respect for the agricultural landscape, incorporating elements of the area's historical background, and a unique personal expression in ornamentation and detailing. The beautiful homes that brand the Napa and Sonoma Valleys with such varied characteristics and idiosyncrasies invoke an innate emotional response; the architecture contributes hugely to the charming atmosphere of the area. This atmosphere of originality and responsible development is an unspoken promise to the wine country that the code of standards will not be broken: these standards note the landowner as a caretaker for a brief period of time. In wine country the land is pervasive and administers a great deal—the land itself requires the residents to be its custodians and protectorates of a way of life.

Wine country shows us a gracious way of living that takes responsibility for the land, and it furnishes us with excellent architectural examples we can incorporate into our lifestyles. To build a home is not only to provide shelter and comfort for our own families, but also to make a contribution to the community and generations to follow. Studying the architecture in wine country, we find inspiration as well as guidelines to help us build a home that will live up to these criteria. Some of these guidelines inform us on individualizing our home, hiring an architect, and deciding on interiors.

Individualizing Your Home

Building or remodeling a home can be one of the most creative processes you can go through to make your world and lifestyle what you want it to be. When your home is an expression of you and your family's way of life, it is more natural for you and your family to have a sense of well-being. To reach the point where a house reflects the attitude of its tenants, you must consider going through a process of discovery.

Contemplate the activities that will take place in the home. You will find out why you are building the house by asking yourself and your family a number of questions:

1. *Is this to be a primary home or a second home?*

   When building a primary residence, living requirements are more utilitarian. When building a second home, the focus may be on relaxation and entertaining as one would experience on a vacation.

2. *Are you building a home to raise children in? If so, how will your home grow to meet the changing needs of children?*

   Perhaps you are a young couple starting a family. Infants and young children have specific safety requirements; fewer stairs prevent accidents, cabinets that lock prevent poisoning, yards that are fenced prevent drowning. In the same way, convenient appliances increase efficiency; closets, shelving, and storage space reduce clutter; certain materials and finishes clean more easily.

3. *Are you retired and planning to entertain?*

   Keep in mind overnight guests. Complete privacy is appreciated both by the visitor and the owner of the home. Schematic layouts will contribute a great deal to the traffic flow in the home. Use thoughtful deliberation to

determine how a space accommodates groups of people in a comfortable way. Understand how you want to direct people through your home. Where would you like them to migrate? Where do you wish to maintain privacy? Will you incorporate outdoor activities with indoor activities? Will the kitchen be the main source of food preparation or will there be an outdoor kitchen for more casual meals? Look into areas where specified activities take place—billiard room, pool house, hot tub, patio, tennis court, and swimming pool. If there are grandchildren, consider the best way to entertain them and occupy their time.

4. *How will you express what inspires you?*

    Keep a file of ideas. Perhaps you have traveled a great deal and have been emotionally impacted by a certain kind of architectural style, a period in history, nuances of a certain culture, a way of life. Colors, textures, and elements may have touched you in a way that feels natural and exhilarating at the same time. Are you a collector of art and sculpture? How will your new home display these works of art? Are you inspired by architectural styles you have seen in magazines—certain details, certain conveniences and attributes? Visits to a friend's home may reveal a detail or two that works with your lifestyle. Home tours showcase new products and techniques for building, interior design, finishes, and textures.

5. *Think carefully about your philosophy of life and what gives you comfort.*

    Do you like to take baths or showers? Are meals family rituals or casual personal choices? Wide-open rooms may be liberating while smaller spaces can provide solace. In which room will you spend most of your time—the bedroom, the study, the kitchen, the family room, or the living room? How do you want the house to interact with nature? Where do you want to orient the view? Do you like formal gardens or natural landscapes?

Once the above information has been explored and precisely articulated, it is time to take the next step.

Hiring an Architect

The architecture in the wine country is the design work of qualified architects who know the area well. The beautiful homes and winery facilities that make up the charming landscape are a result of the expertise and training of designers who share a common goal and maintain a consciousness for their client's needs and the community. Patrons who come prepared with concrete ideas, explore all aspects of their project with a professional, and understand their limitations and goals will be assured satisfaction. It is essential that you take the time to do the proper research to find the right architect for your project. Patience, tenacity, and decisiveness lead to quality architecture that suits the personal needs of the client and the long-term heritage of the community.

The following are several good ways to locate an architect for your project:

1. Check with your local American Institute of Architects (AIA). They will provide a list of local architects in your area. Architects who belong to the AIA are held to professional standards and a code of ethics. These architects use well-trained, qualified contractors with whom they have had experience. A professional architect is informed about the latest technology and has all the resources necessary to complete the job. If you think the services of one of these architects are expensive, you may be dismayed to find out how expensive a nonprofessional turns out to be!

2. Get recommendations from friends and family, and from project managers of structures you admire.

3. Make a list of architects and ask for materials such as websites, brochures,

photographs of recent projects, and fact sheets. Edit your list and begin an interview process.

4. Chemistry is established in an interview. Find out if you are talking the same language as your architect by exploring the questions from your analysis. You must feel that the working relationship will remain comfortable throughout the creative process and the building phase.

5. Talk carefully about your needs, desires, and goals. Be prepared to make adjustments to your desires, as they may not be feasible as the project becomes a reality. Discuss the analysis you have prepared and the personal activity needs of your new home.

6. Discuss the site and the kind of architecture that best suits the footprint of the land you have selected.

7. Discuss budget, fees, and financing the project.

8. Decide whether you want an on-site architect. Some follow the entire process through from beginning to end. Others provide drawings and use project managers to complete the construction administration.

There are several points to consider when working with your architect. While it is important to communicate all your needs, desires, and goals to your architect, understand the point at which you allow your architect to drive the design process.

Points to consider:

1. Allow your architect the time and freedom to give you his or her best work.

2. Be patient with the creative process. Hasty decisions can lead to disappointment.

3. Understand that changes and modifications can be made.

4. Participate in the selection of materials, colors, textures, and lighting fixtures. Know that you have the final say, but also realize that a trained eye sometimes can see things you can't.

5. Contribute resources that you are certain fill the required look you are after.

Deciding on Interiors

Many architectural firms have an interior design department. The interior designers who are part of the firm understand the architects they are working with. They are in tune with the design process and vision of the firm.

Achieving personal expression in an interior design is an issue of paramount importance. Your home is where you will spend your time embraced by rooms that either satisfy or grate. Whether you use the interior design department of your architectural firm, a private interior design company of your own choosing, or do the work yourself, keep in mind compatible interiors and exteriors go hand in hand. You may not want everything to match but understand the fine line between blending color, texture, styles, and accessories requires a keen eye for detail and styling. Personal collections can always be displayed in a way that suits the style of architecture. Home furnishings complete the home and should maintain the same standard as that of the architecture. If a home has been well designed architecturally and well executed in the building phase, yet lacks interior character, it will negate the entire design process.

Wine country is a lesson in thoroughness where quality architecture, finely appointed interiors, and a gracious way of life inspires personal creativity. The Napa and Sonoma Valleys set a standard of taste that can be achieved on a number of levels. While high budget projects have free reign over materials and accouterments, clever design professionals can achieve the desired result a bit more frugally. Regardless of where your project rests within this spectrum, take care to select the appropriate architect, maintain a sensitivity to the context of your building site, keep an awareness of materials and details, and articulate with clarity your needs and desires. In this way, you can turn your dreams into an architectural reality.

Photo by Jessie Whitesides

Resources

Photo by Mary Whitesides

Architects

Backen Gillam Architects
Howard J. Backen
1028 Main St.
St. Helena, CA 94103
Phone: 707.967.1920
Fax: 707.967.1924

BAR Architects
Richard Beard
Ken Linsteadt
Bob Arrigoni
1660 Bush St.
San Francisco, CA 94109
Phone: 415.441.4771
Fax: 415.536.2323

BCV Architects
Hans Baldauf
Ken Calton
Chris Von Eckartsberg
1527 Stockton St.
San Francisco, CA 94133
Phone: 415.398.6538

Walker-Moody Architects
Sandy Walker
2666 Hyde St.
San Francisco, CA 94109-1221
Phone: 415.885.0800

Brandenberg Taylor Lombardo Architects LLP
Maurice Lombardo
74 New Montgomery St.
Suite 740
San Francisco, CA 94105
Phone: 415.243.4474
Fax: 415.243.4411
www.btl-arch.com

Jim Jennings, Architect
25 Brush Place
San Francisco, CA 94103
Phone: 415.551.0827

Walker Warner Architects
Brooks Walker
Greg Warner
835 Terry Francois St.
San Francisco, CA 94107
Phone: 415.318.8907 (Brooks)
Phone: 415.318.8908 (Greg)
www.walker-warner.com

Architectural Resources Group
Pier 9 The Embarcadero
San Francisco, CA 94111
Phone: 415.421.1680
Fax: 415.421.0127
E-mail: arg@argsf.com

Ron Nunn, Architect
300 Taplin Road
St. Helena, CA 94574
Phone: 707.963.0899

Landscape Architects

SWA Group
John Loomis
2200 Bridgeway Blvd.
P.O. Box 5904
Sausalito, CA 94966-5904
Phone: 415.332.5100

Townsend Landscaping
Napa, Valley
Phone: 707.967.9600
Fax: 707.967.0918

Jack Chandler & Associates
P.O. Box 2180
Yountville, CA 94599
Phone: 707.944.8352
Fax: 707.944.0651
E-mail: jcal1870@earthlink.net

Contractors

James Nolan Construction
P.O. Box 90
St. Helena, CA 94574
Phone: 707.963.3222
Fax: 707.963.3828

Koala Development Corp.
P.O. Box 218
Rutherford, CA 94573
Phone: 707.963.7027
Fax: 707.963.6792

Jim Murphy and Associates
464 Kenwood Court #B
Santa Rosa, CA 95407
Phone: 707.576.7337
Fax: 707.576.7173

Interior Design

Barbara Colvin & Co. Design
1350 Yount Mill Road
Napa, CA 94558
Phone: 415.602.1233

Les Poisson Interiors
Ken Poisson
25 N. Santa Cruz Ave.
Los Gados, CA 95030
Phone: 408.354.7937; 707.486.0939

Candra Scott and Anderson
Interior Design
2009 17th St.
San Francisco, CA
Phone: 415.861.0690

Babey Moulton Jue and Booth
Interior Design
416 2nd Street
#C 127
San Francisco, CA 94103
Phone: 415.979.9880

Fisher Weisman Design & Decoration
Jeffry Weisman
616 Minna Street
San Francisco, CA 94103
Phone: 415.255.2254
Fax: 415.255.1254

SDH Design
Jacques Saint Dizier ASID
259 Center St.
Healdsburg, CA
Phone: 707.472.9080
Fax: 707.472.0981
www.sdhdesign.com

Carter LaRoche, Architect
Trina LaRoche, Interior Designer
181 Winslow Way
Suite F
Bainbridge Island, WA 98110
Phone: 206.842.2528
www.mlrarchitects.com

Napa and Sonoma Valley Wineries

Quintessa
Joyce Christine Stavert
Director of Consumer Relations
1601 Silverado Trail
Rutherford, CA 94573
Phone: 707.967.1601
Fax: 707.286.2727

Mumm Napa Valley Winery
Kathy McClure
Hospitality Director
P.O. Drawer 500
Rutherford, CA 94573
Phone: 800.686.6222

Viansa Winery
25200 Arnold Drive
Sonoma, CA 95476
Phone: 707.935.4700
Fax: 707.996.4632
www.viansa.com

Far Niente
The Napa Valley Estate
Mary Marshall Grace
Director of Communications
P.O. Box 327
Oakville, CA 94562
Phone: 707.944.2861
Fax: 707.944.2312

Franciscan Oakville Estate
Highway 29 at Galleron Road
St. Helena, CA 94103
Phone: 800.529.WINE, ext. 73830
www.Franciscan.com

Nickel & Nickel
Highway 29
Oakville, CA
Phone: 707.967.9600
Fax: 707.967.0918

Maple Lane Vineyards
Michael & Toni Doilney
Calistoga, CA
Phone: 707.486.1100
E-mail: doilney@maplelanevineyards.com

Home Furnishings and Materials

Rustic Stuff
Karen Roberts
Paul Faulk
15040 N. Northsight Blvd.
Suite #102
Scottsdale, AZ 89260
Interior design
Antiques from around the world

By the Square
Colleen
521 B – Broadway
Sonoma, CA 95476
Phone: 707.996.5600
Fax: 707.996.5515
E-mail: colleen@pjs2go.com
Asian-influenced interiors and
furnishings

Jot em Down Antiques
613 Hwy 80 East
Sunnyvale, Texas 75182
Phone: 972.226.0974
E-mail: info@jot-emdown.com
European antiques

Authentique
242 Main Street
Alpine, Utah 84004
Phone: 877.4FRANCE
Fax: 801.756.7646
Antique French imports

David Brower Antiques
114 Kensington Church Street
Kensington, London W8 7LN
England
Phone: 1-44 (0) 20 7221-4155
Fax: 1-44 (0) 20 7221-6211
E-mail: enquiries@davidbrowerantiques.com
www.davidbrower-antiques.com
European antiques and architectural salvage

European Antiques LLC
Michael Oserianski
53 Heatherwood Dr.
Madison, CT 06443
Phone: 203.421.5193
E-mail: antiques@european-antiques-llc.com
www.european-antiques-llc.com
Large selection of European antique
furniture & accessories

Eron Johnson Antiques Ltd.
451 Broadway
Denver, CO 80203
Phone: 303.777.8700
Fax: 303.777.8787
E-mail: eron@eronjohnsonantiques.com
www.eron@eronjohnsonantiques.com
Excellent architectural salvage elements and
antique furniture

From France 2 You
Phone: 866.205.0767
Fax: 301.231.9736
E-mail: michelle@fromfrance2you.com
www.fromfrance2you.com
Authentic French antique furniture, architectural
salvage elements and paintings

France Antiques
Isle-sur-la Sorgue
84800 France
E-mail: info@franceantiques.com
www.antiques-cdarts.com

J. Tribble Antiques
764 Miami Circle NE #122
Atlanta, GA 30324
Phone: 888.652.6116; 404.846.1156
Fax: 404.846.1179
E-mail: jtribbleantiques@mindspring.com
www.jtribbleantiques.com
Bauhaus modern antiques

Modern Classics
European Furniture Importers
2145 W. Grand Ave.
Chicago, IL 60612
Phone: 800.243.1955
www.eurofurniture.com
Modern classic furniture from Europe

Antiques on Old Plank Road
331 East Ogden Ave.
Westmont, IL 60559
Phone: 630.887.1995
www.oldplank.com
Broad selection of antiques including Bauhaus

Asian Essence
Phone: 773.782.9500
E-mail: dste@asianessence.com
www.asianessence.com
Full selection of Asian furniture

Atmosphere
2174 Union Street
San Francisco, CA 94123-4004
Phone: 415.614.1097; 415.614.1697
Contemporary furniture and accessories

Therapy
541 Valencia Street
San Francisco, CA 94110-1114
Phone: 415.621.5902
Contemporary retro furniture and accessories

Linn
290 Townsend Street
San Francisco, CA 94107-1719
Phone: 415.643.5466
Contemporary accessories

Interior Materials

Ann Sacks
2 Henry Adams St. #125
San Francisco, CA 94103
Phone: 415.252.5889
Fax: 415.252.5911
www.annsacks.com
Exotic tiles for floors and counters

Mountain Lumber
Phone: 800.445.2671; 434.985.3646
Fax: 434.985.4105
E-mail: sales@mountainlumber.com
www.mountainlumber.com
Recycled lumber

Yesteryear Floorwoods Company
Suite 6 2331 East Market Street
York, PA 17402
Phone: 800.233.9307; 717.840.0330
Fax: 717.840.1408
www.agedwoods.com
Recycled woods for flooring

Chestnut Woodworking & Antique
  Flooring Co. LLC
Bob Friedman
West Cornwall, CT 06796
Phone: 860.672.4300
Fax: 860.672.2441
E-mail: info@chestnutwoodworking.com
www.chestnutwoodworking.com
Recycled flooring

Whiskey Wood Company
3658 State Road
Hartford, KY 42347
Phone: 270.298.0084
Fax: 271.298.7755
www.whiskeywoods.com
Recycled woods

Bois Chamois
903 Creek Rd.
Kennett Square, PA 19348
Phone: 610.444.0583
Fax: 610.925.4659
E-mail: Richard@boischamois.com
www.boischamois.com
Vintage hardwood flooring

The Barn People
Windsor, VT
Phone: 802.674.5898
Fax: 802.674.6310
www.thebarnpeople.com
Dismantling old structures—
  Nickel & Nickel Winery

BM Barnsiding
Monroe, NY
Phone: 800.499.0444; 845.783.1059
Fax: 845.783.9471
www.theatricalprops.com

Carlson's Barnwood Company
Cambridge, IL
Phone: 309.522.5550
Fax: 309.522.5123
www.Carlsonsbarnwood.com

Vintage Beams and Timber Inc.
P.O. Box 548
Sylva, NC 28779
Phone: 828.586.0755
Fax: 828.586.4647
E-mail: info@vintagebeamsandtimbers.com
www.vintagebeamsandtimbers.com
Old brick pavers from China, old trusses, and
other miscellaneous items

Caldwells
195 Bayshore Blvd.
San Francisco, CA 94124
Phone: 415.550.6777
Fax: 415.550.0249
www.caldwell-bldg-salvage.com
The building salvage resource

Eden Garden Antiques
Kiln Croft
Skelton, Penrith
Cumoria Call 9SQ UK
Phone: 01 7684 84026
Fax: 01 7684 84051
E-mail: john@edenreclaim.demon.co.uk
www.demolitions.co.uk
Excellent reclaimed architectural elements

Georges Pougin Antiques
Grand Route 83
Bourdon 6990
Marche en Famenne, France
Phone: 0032 (0) 84 34 24 7
Architectural salvage

Photo by Jessie Whitesides

Photography Credits

Richard Barnes, 64

Mark Darley, 163, 166

Doug Dun, BAR Architects, 95, 96, 122, 124, 125, 129, 130, 132, 133, 135, 144, 146, 147, 148, 149, 150, 151

Courtesy of Far Niente, 85, 87

Glen Graves, 70, 72

J. D. Peterson, 16, 157, 159, 160, 161, 164, 165

Erhard Pfeiffer, 19, 20, 152, 154, 158, 162, 167, 168, 173

Tim Street Porter, 126, 127, 128

Jessie Whitesides, 176, 178, 181, 182, 184

Mary Whitesides, ii, 10, 17, 22, 23, 24, 26, 31, 32, 33, 35, 36, 40, 44, 45, 46, 49, 52, 60, 63, 72, 80, 86, 88, 100, 102, 103, 106, 109, 119, 120, 136, 137, 138, 139, 141, 174, 177

Photo by Jessie Whitesides